HIDDEN
HISTORY
of
LAKE COUNTY
OHIO

HIDDEN
HISTORY
of
LAKE COUNTY
OHIO

Jennifer Boresz Engelking

THE
Hi$tory
PRESS

Published by The History Press
Charleston, SC
www.historypress.com

Front cover: Postcard showing beach and pavilions at Willoughbeach Amusement Park, early 1900s. *Courtesy of Willoughby Historical Society. Restoration by Jim Dudash, Dudash Factory. Back cover*: Fairport Harbor West Breakwater Lighthouse at sunset. *Photo by Andrew Cross, AC Aerial Photography.*

First published 2021

Manufactured in the United States

ISBN 9781467144582

Library of Congress Control Number: 2020951870

To my family and friends.

To the history-makers and history-preservers of Lake County.

CONTENTS

Preface   9
Acknowledgements   11

1. Early Days   13
2. Maritime History   30
3. Unique Structures   53
4. War Heroes   75
5. Notable Residents   91
6. Agriculture and Industry   105
7. Schools and Education   123
8. Parks and Recreation   143
9. Nearly Lost and Threatened   160
10. Legends, Myths and Discoveries   178

Epilogue   197
Bibliography   199
About the Author   207

PREFACE

The waves gently lap the shoreline as I walk along the beach with my parents. When you're a child, Lake Erie is full of secrets waiting to be discovered. I look for beach glass shining on the sand, but hope to find a long-lost piece of treasure, fallen from a pirate ship that once sailed its waters.

Fast-forward many years, and I am walking the beach with my own children, watching them excitedly search for hidden treasure, like a weathered marble that, in their eyes, is as valuable as gold. The thrill of the treasure hunt has stayed with me through the years, but now I realize treasure comes in all forms, and sometimes, the greatest worth doesn't come from finding a lost object but from discovering a story nearly lost to time.

I realize the important role Lake Erie has played across generations. The great ships and steamboats' tales of triumph and tragedy helped develop Lake County's industrial and recreational foundation and inspired imaginations for centuries.

Although the county was named after it, Lake Erie is only one piece of its hidden history. Lake County is filled with fascinating stories, some that became legendary and are only known in bits and pieces, woven through time by friends sitting around a campfire or neighbors comparing notes about what their community used to be like. For me, it's those missing pieces that are so intriguing.

I wanted to write this book to fill in some of the gaps, and I hope readers will find that the stories inside are like pieces of lost Lake County treasure.

The biggest challenge was deciding what to include because our county is overflowing with history hiding in plain sight. I choose stories of fearless leaders and explorers, pivotal events and groundbreaking architecture that have made our county what it is today, and I hope reading it will inspire you to seek out more stories in your own community. I might not be a trained historian, but I'm a lifelong Lake County resident who loves getting to the heart of a good story—the story behind the story. It's been a pleasure meeting so many people who are passionate about our county's history, and I am honored to have the opportunity to share their stories with you. I hope you enjoy reading them as much as I have enjoyed researching them.

ACKNOWLEDGEMENTS

I would like to thank my commissioning editor, John Rodrigue, for his guidance and expertise throughout this journey, along with everyone at The History Press, who helped transform my stories into a book. I am truly grateful to work with such professionals.

I'm thankful for the help of so many people in the community who have generously shared their time and resources with me, especially the historians at our local libraries and historical societies: Alan Hitchcox and Pat Lewis (Willoughby), Gale Lippucci (Willowick), Marje Shook (Madison), Kathy Suglia (Wickliffe), Marie Tomko (Eastlake) and Lori Watson (Leroy).

Thank you to the following, who have contributed information and/or photos: Caitlin Ambrose, Dr. Todd Arrington, Margot Baldwin, Bill Barrow, Katherine Behnke, M. Joanne Boresz, Kristin Brewster Goodell, Bob Buescher, Kirsten Bull, Bill Burk, Sheila Consaul, Jaime Cordova, Elaine Crane, Andrew Cross, Beth Debevc, Summer DeMore Boresz, Jim Dudash, Korene Engelking, Greg Eyler, David Gartner, Mark Gilson, Katherine Harris Szerdy, Sharon Hill, the owners of Hilo Farm, Brian Horgan, Pat Huebner, Joan Kapsch, Tom Kimball, Ron Kotar, Lisa Lynch, Judy MacKeigan, Dan Maxson, Mark Petzing, Elizabeth Piwkowski, Lisa Potti, Ted Prindle, Ken Reeves, Debra Remington, Deanna and Fred Rowe, Lori Roy, Marguerite "Muffi" Sherwin, Bill Smith, Nick Standering, May Targett, Dr. Laura Tradowsky, Brenda Traffis, Cathi Weber, Sue Wovrosh, the Willo Beach Park Association, Linda Zinn and Peggy Zirbes.

Special thanks to Deanna R. Adams, Wendy Hoke and Joseph Koskovics for your support with my book and throughout my writing career.

Most of all, I would like to thank my wonderful family and friends for their unwavering love and support. Thank you to my lifelong friends Beth Cattell, Heather Husted, Kristin Petruziello and Adrian Shaw for always encouraging me. Thank you to my parents, Joanne and Dale Boresz, for instilling in me a love of reading and writing very early on and for always believing I could do it, and to Mary Ann and Dave Engelking, for cheering me on. Thank you to my amazing husband, Brian, and our three incredible children. Your love motivates me each day.

EARLY DAYS

Rolling farms stretch across Lake County, Ohio. New and historic neighborhoods dot its landscape. The waves of Lake Erie curl across about thirty miles of beaches on the county's north end, where lighthouses stand as stately reminders of its past.

Lake County might be the smallest county in the state geographically, encompassing only 228.2 square miles, but it's filled with an abundance of colorful history and intriguing legends.

In fact, its size almost prevented it from becoming a county. When pioneers in Painesville (part of Geauga County and the largest town in the Reserve with 1,257 people) tired of traveling to the county seat in northern Geauga, they decided to create Lake County using part of Geauga and Cuyahoga Counties. They met with opposition because the area they proposed didn't meet the minimum size requirements to become a county. Then they discovered original surveyor maps, showing that part of the land was actually under Lake Erie. So, on March 6, 1840, Lake County was created, with around two-thirds of its land lying under the lake.

Lake Erie was created some twenty thousand years ago when a massive glacier moving down from the north wore off mountain peaks, filled in valleys, left behind rich soil and formed the Great Lakes. The carved-out waterways have played pivotal roles in the region's business and recreation throughout the centuries.

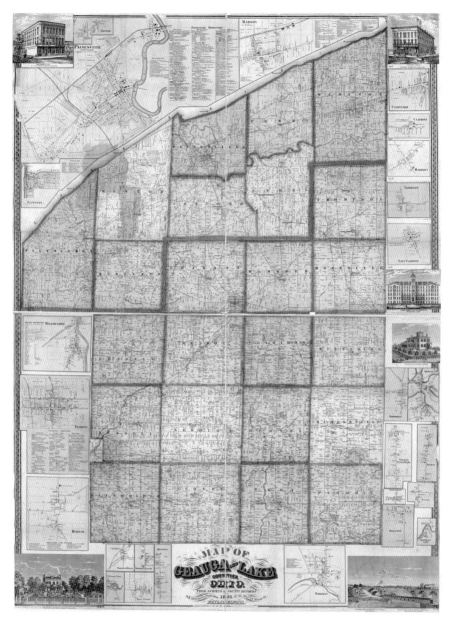

An 1857 map of Geauga and Lake Counties. *Courtesy of Library of Congress.*

First Inhabitants

The first human inhabitants in Ohio arrived around 13,000 BC, first the Paleo-Indians, then archaic man and eventually the mound builders. The highly developed society grew crops and made tools and weapons, many of which have been found in the animal-shaped mounds they built to bury their dead. Mounds have been discovered throughout the county, although most were leveled by farmers settling the region.

Whittlesey Tradition

The Whittlesey Tradition lived in Lake County from about AD 900 to 1650. It was named after geologist Colonel Charles Whittlesey, who discovered their sites throughout Ohio.

One of the county's most important Whittlesey sites is the Reeves Village Site, which is about a quarter mile south of the mouth of the Chagrin River (called Shagrin by Native Americans, meaning "clear water"). Many artifacts found at the site have been given to museums, including the Indian Museum of Lake County.

Although Native Americans first occupied this land, the French followed and built a trade post called Charlton at the mouth of the river as early as 1750. They left the area after being defeated by the English in the French and Indian War. In 1796, surveyor Charles Parker built his cabin (possibly the first house in Willoughby Township) and several huts at the mouth of the river for Connecticut Land Company surveyors.

Another major Whittlesey site is in Fairport Harbor, about three-quarters of a mile from Lake Erie, south of the railroad crossing on East Street. Thousands of items, like storage pots, arrowheads and chisels, were found at the edge of a bluff overlooking the Grand River valley, called Geauga or Sheauga by Native Americans, believed to have meant "raccoon river." (The French called it LaGrande Riviere.)

The Grand River provided entry into the Western Reserve for many settlers, including Connecticut Land Company land agent Turhand Kirtland, who arrived at the mouth of the river in 1798. He went on to blaze a trail to Burton that became an important artery in the development of the frontier and became a large landholder in Kirtland Township, which was named after him.

Photo. only, Copyright 1905 by the Rotograph Co.
A 4524 Looking down Grand River, Painesville, O

Postcard of Grand River in Painesville, 1905. *Author's collection.*

MAPPING THE WESTERN RESERVE

Just over two centuries ago, bustling towns like Willoughby and Painesville were only dense forests covering the county in a canopy of green. The forest was said to be so lush that squirrels never had to touch the ground.

The land, known as the Western Reserve, can be traced back to land grants made to the colonies by England's King Charles II in 1662. After the Revolutionary War, states were encouraged to give up their claims to these western lands to create the Northwest Territory, which became Connecticut's Western Reserve, so that the land could be sold to finance the newly independent country.

A group of investors, forming the Connecticut Land Company, bought more than three million acres of land at forty cents an acre. They chose Moses Cleaveland, investor and director of the Connecticut Land Company, to lead a party of fifty-one surveyors to determine their assets and establish north–south range lines sectioned into five-mile-square townships so that the land could be sold.

Cleaveland's group, including an astronomer, cook, physician and boatman, first set foot at the mouth of Conneaut Creek on July 4, 1796, after sixty-eight days of travel. They celebrated their arrival to the Western Reserve, and the country's birth, by firing a federal salute of fifteen rounds, plus one, in honor of New Connecticut. They made toasts, drinking two pails of grog, a mixture of rum and water flavored with lemon, sugar and spices.

Surveyors were on their way to the Cuyahoga River to lay out a new city (later named Cleveland, dropping the *a* after it was misprinted in publication). They rejoiced when they thought they reached the mouth of the Cuyahoga but quickly learned from Native Americans that it was in fact the Chagrin River and they were still one day's journey away. Their disappointment and chagrin, noted in surveyors' journals, has led to speculation that the river was named after their emotions at that false moment of discovery.

Another theory, as noted on Ohio Historical Society commemorative markers, suggests the river was named after eighteenth century French fur trader Francois Sieur de Saquin (or Saguine), who built a trading post at the

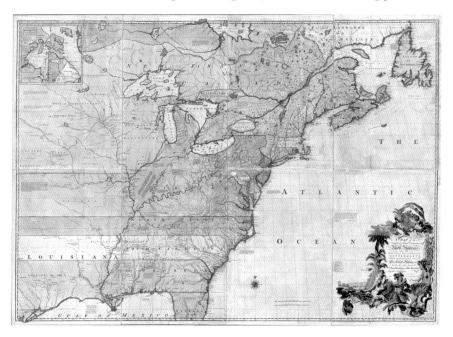

A 1755 map of the British and French dominions in North America. *Courtesy of Library of Congress.*

mouth of the Cuyahoga River and likely crossed to the Chagrin River when trading with Native Americans.

After months of hardship, the Connecticut Land Company realized it couldn't map out the entire Western Reserve in one summer and returned east in the fall of 1796, carrying expertly surveyed maps.

A second expedition, sent to complete the survey in 1797, discovered its territory holdings were only two and a half million acres instead of three million acres because the rest was underwater in Lake Erie.

Pioneers quickly realized the land, though primitive, was a prime location to establish their homes. It had rich soil for agriculture, plentiful rivers for mills and transportation, forests filled with timber and Lake Erie to transport goods and people. The land company wasted no time in promoting sales, and the clear property lines it created are the basis for today's land abstracts, with property deeds referring back to the original range, township and tract designations.

Trails and Roads

Girdled Road

In 1797, a route was proposed from the Cuyahoga River to the western Pennsylvania line, parallel to and south of what is now U.S. Route 20. A year later, Connecticut Land Company directors signed a $2,600 contract with General Simon Perkins to cut a one-hundred-mile road with bridges over streams too deep to ford, which would become Old Girdled Road.

Its name was derived from "girdling" (or encircling cuts) through tree bark, causing the tree to die, which made felling easier. It was a common practice among Native Americans and pioneers.

The road, following the Native American middle ridge trail, passed through Ashtabula, Geauga and Lake Counties before heading westward to Cleveland via Euclid Avenue. A camp for surveyors constructing the road, set up where Girdled Road crosses the Painesville-Chardon Highway, became known as Perkins' construction camp. The only remaining remnants of Girdled Road are in Concord and Leroy Townships.

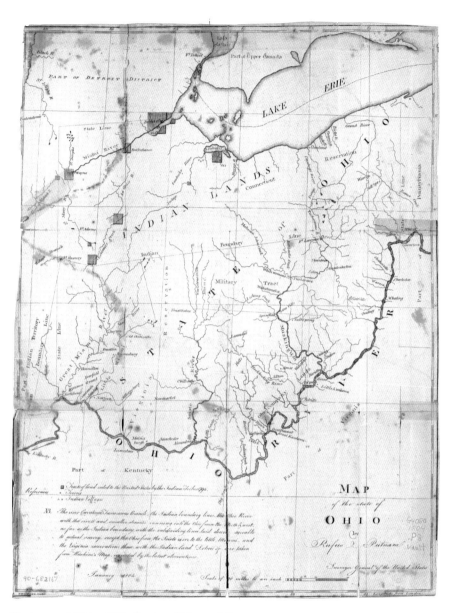

First map of Ohio, 1805. *Courtesy of Library of Congress.*

Indian Trails

Additional roads were forged as the need increased for settlers to reach family and friends and access mills. State Route 84 was cut along the Indian trail to connect some of the settlements. By 1802, the Indian path from Abbott's Mill to Grand River, which was a wagon trace, was starting to transition into a busier route, eventually becoming Mentor Avenue.

The city of Mentor itself is believed to be named after early settler Hiram Mentor, although a map of the Western Reserve, predating settlers, shows several townships in range nine engraved as Mentor. It could be from ancient Greek literature, as Mentor was the tutor of Telemachus, son of Odysseus.

Ohio became a state in 1803 but was still a vast territory of dense forests and rugged ravines that made travel challenging.

The paths settlers used to reach the eastern lake shore of the Reserve were actually Indian trails and paths created by the movement of animals. The Lake Trail connected Buffalo to Painesville, with Euclid Avenue now

Corner of Vine Street and Lakeshore Boulevard, 1905. *Courtesy of Willoughby Historical Society.*

almost directly on it. River Road, which meets Euclid Avenue in Downtown Willoughby, follows another Indian trail, known as the Salt Trail, because salt was "imported" along the trail. It was important for Native Americans' food and to treat animal hides.

Lakeshore Boulevard, once just trading and transportation trails, hugs the shore of Lake Erie from the west end of Willowick into Mentor. Although it is one of the county's busiest roads, it was once so narrow that two cars couldn't pass each other.

On the corner of Lakeshore Boulevard and East 288th Street, in Willowick, sits a restaurant, The Cabin of Willowick, a remnant of its earlier days. In the 1880s, it was a hunting lodge and became a popular restaurant in the 1930s. Although it's been ravished by several fires, its original fieldstone fireplace has survived and continues to warm guests.

Vine Street, in Willowick, was once a crooked dirt road, and Willowick Drive, from Vine to East 305th Street, was known as Return Avenue because road conditions were so bad that travelers had to return because they couldn't go further.

Mail and Stagecoaches

As settlers arrived, mail and passenger transport soon followed and the first mail carrier, a man named McIllvain (published with varying spellings), made 150-mile trips by foot across the Reserve once a week. The main route at this time was along the barely passable Buffalo-Cleveland Road, now U.S. Route 20. The only access to the settlement from the east was by horse or stagecoach passing through water in an old Indian ford.

By 1808, another early mail carrier, John Metcalf, delivered mail by foot over a route stretching from Erie to Cleveland. He even swam across streams, holding his mailbag high above his head to keep its contents dry, to deliver the mail to various stations with surprising punctuality. Postage in 1813 was up to twenty-five cents per letter.

By 1823, two decades after the establishment of the first coach line, mail coach service began in Lake County. The terrible road conditions— thick with trees and brush, swamps and streams—continued to make mail delivery challenging.

The earliest roads were poorly maintained and often impassable, especially in the rainy months of spring. To combat that problem, corduroy roads were built through the low, wet places. These were made by laying poles across the road, but the timber quickly rotted. Next early builders tried plank roads, laying heavy sills along the direction of the road and covering them with planks laid across (ten to twelve feet wide).

Eventually, a narrow bridge was built at the future Pelton Road, allowing more people to build a new life in Chagrin.

By the 1830s, a regular stage route was created between Cleveland and Buffalo. The trip between the cities took two days and two nights, with stops at stations along the way, including Wickliffe, Painesville and Unionville. A stagecoach could hold up to ten passengers, along with mail sacks tucked beneath the driver boots and luggage stored in the boot behind or strapped to the roof.

The hardworking horses pulling the coaches across uneven terrain were changed every ten miles. Inns began popping up along the route, providing a room and breakfast in the morning. Between 1830 and 1850, a tavern breakfast often included ham, beefsteak, fried potatoes, griddle cakes and coffee. Among the most famous were Ye Old Tavern in Unionville, Rider Tavern in Painesville and Lloyd Tavern in Wickliffe. The first two still exist today.

Unionville Tavern

In 1798, a small log cabin was built in the settlement village known as Unionville, providing temporary housing for settlers who arrived when the Connecticut Land Company opened an office nearby. It quickly became known as a resting spot for weary travelers and a social center for settling pioneers. At just twelve by fifteen feet, with windows covered in greased paper and walls covered in mud, it was one of the original cabins in the Reserve.

In 1803, it was designated as a stop on the first mail route between Cleveland and Warren. A second cabin, an exact duplicate of the first, was added later, and both were connected by a roof. The building known today as the Unionville Tavern was built in the early 1820s. It is a two-story saltbox house of the two log cabins, with a covered carriage entrance and a second-floor ballroom. For years, it served two stagecoach lines at its junction of the main Cleveland-Buffalo route and the road from Harper's landing to Warren. It became a place for cattle drivers to rest, along with Arcola iron workers, sailors and workers from Madison Dock.

Unionville Tavern, Historic American Buildings Survey, 1933. *Courtesy of Library of Congress.*

Guest meals, cooked in the big stone fireplace in a room serving as both kitchen and dining room, included fish, game, vegetables and fruit. An 1845 ledger quoted $1.50 for breakfast, dinner and overnight lodging for a man and team of horses.

By the mid-1800s, the tavern was serving as a stop on the Underground Railroad. It's believed that enslaved people escaped through tunnels leading from an empty grave in the Harpersfield Cemetery, under what is now State Route 84, into the basement of the tavern and then out through the field behind the building.

Over the last two centuries, the tavern has been known by a variety of names—first the Webster House. In the mid-nineteenth century, it was the New England House and later Ye Olde Tavern. During most of the twentieth century, it was known as the Old Tavern.

Brian Horgan is vice-president of operations for the Unionville Tavern Preservation Society, which is a group of volunteers restoring the Old Tavern to the grandeur of its early days. He says you can see from the basement that the tunnels do angle out toward the southeast corner in the direction of the cemetery, but the preservation society hasn't explored the tunnel space yet. They are pursuing funding for an archaeological exploration of the area to protect and preserve the tunnels.

There are plenty of legends surrounding the Old Tavern. For example, the author of *Uncle Tom's Cabin*, Harriet Beecher Stowe, is believed to have visited the historic site, where runaway slave and abolitionist Milton Clarke was rescued from bounty hunters by locals.

Clarke was from Kentucky and was living in Oberlin when he went to Madison in 1843 to speak at an abolition rally. The next day, while out walking, he was captured and beaten by slave catchers.

While being transported eastward, his wagon was stopped in front of the Old Tavern by abolitionists from Lake and Ashtabula Counties, including the Ashtabula sheriff. The sheriff took Clarke into custody, and while being taken to the county jail, Clarke mysteriously escaped. He and his brother, Lewis, later crossed paths with Stowe while continuing their speaking tour, and it's theorized that she was so inspired by their story that she incorporated it into the character of George in *Uncle Tom's Cabin*.

Another feature possibly linked to its role as an Underground Railroad station is a narrow stairway in the back of the building, leading up from the basement. Since it was out of public view, it might have been used as a servants' stairway that also provided enslaved people an entrance to small boarding rooms on the upper floors. Other homes in the area also have interesting features, like false spaces that could have allowed for similar activity.

By the early 1900s, the tavern was in a severe state of disrepair and underwent a significant renovation, reopening to the public around 1914.

Many famous people visited, including Henry Ford and Thomas Edison, who vacationed in the area during the summer. James R. Garfield, son of the president and the secretary of the interior for President Theodore Roosevelt, is believed to have dined at the tavern, along with A.M. Willard, painter of the famous painting *Spirit of '76*.

The Old Tavern officially closed in 2006 and sat vacant for eight years. In 2011, the Unionville Tavern Preservation Society was established, following the success of a grassroots preservation campaign, and acquired the property in 2014. It has been raising funds to stabilize and restore the building and historic gardens, but it's a race against time to preserve a piece of history full of memories for locals.

It's believed to be the oldest tavern in the state of Ohio and was added to the National Register of Historic Places in 1973. It was listed on Preservation Ohio's Most Endangered Historic Sites list from 2012 to 2014 and is the only such identified historic building the organization has declared "saved" after just three years.

Left: Harriet Beecher Stowe, 1880. *Courtesy of Library of Congress.*

Below: Postcard of the Old Tavern dining room, 1947. *Author's collection.*

During extensive stabilization work, society preservationists discovered several interesting artifacts. In the ballroom, a 1930s business card from a musician who likely performed at the tavern was embedded in a door jam. Also, a butter churner was revealed inside a wall when repairs were being made. It is believed to be part of a time capsule waiting to be discovered. Lowell Keairns, the grandson of Arthur and Hulda Fritze, tavern owners from 1926 to 1946, has provided the group with information, stories and memorabilia, including china and old photos. He donated an arrow that his grandfather allowed him to take as a memento when the property sold after World War II. A previous owner told Mr. Fritz that the arrow stood in the garden as a signal to runaway slaves. When it was pointed north, it was safe to enter the tunnel. Horgan says the society looks forward to placing the arrow back in its original location once restorations are completed.

As of this writing, the Old Tavern remains closed to the public during restorations, which are dependent on volunteers, grants and donations from the community. Little did those early builders know that they were laying the foundation for a pivotal piece of our region's history and creating a special gathering place that would span several historic eras of significance, remaining at the heart of the community for over two hundred years.

The Unionville Tavern Preservation Society works tirelessly to "Save the Tavern!" because it is not only preserving history but also saving a landmark filled with memories of marriage proposals, weddings, special birthdays and anniversaries with the hope that it will once again become a gathering place for future generations.

RIDER'S INN

Rider's Inn, in Painesville, has been a Lake County institution for more than two hundred years. It was built by Joseph Rider, who walked five hundred miles in 1802 to inspect his newly purchased eight hundred acres of land in the Western Reserve. After building a cabin and returning east to bring his wife and three daughters to the cabin, he opened Rider's Tavern on June 16, 1812, on the old Indian trail between Cleveland and Buffalo, also believed to be part of the busy Oregon Trail.

According to Elaine Crane, current owner of Rider's Inn, Rider rushed to build it before the start of the War of 1812 so that soldiers would have somewhere to stay. She said army soldiers gathered at the inn as they prepared to join Admiral Oliver Hazard Perry's troops for the Battle of Lake Erie.

An 1812 map of Ohio. *Courtesy of Library of Congress.*

When stagecoaches began stopping, the restaurant and inn often had 150 guests a night, and to direct even more business to his inn from the South Ridge traffic rather than to his rivals, Rider cut a road through the woods from his tavern to the Warren Road. He put a sign up at the river stating, "This Way to Only Tavern." That road has become Walnut Street in Painesville, and although business did increase at Rider's Tavern, so did that of his nearby rivals.

The inn became a retreat for returning Union Civil War soldiers, along with an important stop on the Underground Railroad for thousands of enslaved people. The escaping enslaved people knew to watch for a light in the uppermost southern part of the building, and if it was on, they knew they could find refuge. They entered through a wishing well and hid in the basement until they got the signal that it was OK to stealthily travel through the tunnels to the ships on Lake Erie that were waiting to take them to freedom in Canada. Although the tunnels are unsafe to go in today, they add to the authenticity that designated Rider's Inn as an official stop on the Underground Railroad. Over the years, Crane and her staff have found a number of artifacts from the inn's early years, like a handmade musket in what would have been an outhouse in the tunnels, a lantern that would have been used to light a window and artwork depicting enslaved people drawn on music paper.

In recent years, Rider's Inn has even offered special programs, including a replicated slave meal, to immerse visitors in the life they lived.

Over the years, the inn has gone through several structural changes. Esteemed Western Reserve architect Jonathan Goldsmith enlarged the tavern in 1822 and built a large portico across the front with six square boxed-in pillars along the veranda, with weight-bearing timbers of walnut inside each one. It's said that Joseph Rider's son Zerah, who was twelve years old at the time, hauled these timbers from nearby Blackbrook Marsh. Goldsmith also raised the roof and added a second story.

Rider Tavern, Historic American Buildings Survey, 1933. *Courtesy of Library of Congress.*

When Joseph Rider died in 1840, Zerah (one of his nineteen children) and his wife, Louisa Perkins, took over tavern operations. According to *Jonathan Goldsmith: Pioneer Master Builder in the Western Reserve*, Zerah recalled in his later years how busy the tavern was at its peak: "I remember standing on the veranda and counting one hundred wagons and ox-carts passing in the road or standing near the tavern. People slept in the halls and on the floors and outside under their wagons."

He also described the ballroom that began at the west end and covered about two-thirds of the second floor, with handmade wooden benches lining the floor and an eight-inch-high and eight-foot-long platform. It was lit by coal oil lamps held to the wall by brackets.

"My father loved to give dances," Zerah said. "I used to pull a bale of hay along the floor to polish it while my father pushed. I have seen my six sisters dancing on the floor many a time."

The Rider family sold the inn in 1902, when it fell on hard times. George Randall was the next owner and bought it in 1922, after the discovery of a short-lived hot spring. He added a dining room, opened a speakeasy during Prohibition and enlarged the traditional Sunday Stagecoach Breakfast. The Lutz brothers were the next owners, in 1940, and ran the inn for several decades. Then Elaine Crane and her mother, Elizabeth Roemisch, bought it in the 1980s. They completely refurbished it into a beautiful country inn, and Elaine is still running it today.

Rider's Tavern, now known as Rider's Inn, has remained in business for more than two centuries, thanks to owners who understood the importance of preserving its history.

OTHER TAVERNS

Lloyd's Tavern, in Wickliffe, was another famous tavern, built of brick made on the grounds and an interior finished with hand-carved woodwork. It was the first stop out of Cleveland to change horses, which made it very prosperous during the stagecoach years. It was knocked down in 1949 to make way for retail stores.

There were many other inns in Lake County from 1815 to 1860. Jesse Ladd's Tavern, built in 1812 on South Ridge Road in Madison Township, flourished as a tavern until 1827. It's listed on the National Register of Historic Places and is still standing today as multifamily apartments.

2

Maritime History

Sinking of the *G.P. Griffith*

On warm, summer evenings at Lakefront Lodge, Willowick residents enjoy sweeping views of Lake Erie as the sun sinks below the horizon, leaving behind brushstrokes of pink, orange and deep purple across the sky. It's hard to imagine such an idyllic setting was once the site of one of the greatest tragedies on the Great Lakes.

On June 16, 1850, the three-year-old steamboat *G.P. Griffith* departed Buffalo, New York, on a three-day trip to Toledo. The six-hundred-ton, 192-foot side-wheeler was named after businessman Griffith P. Griffith and constructed in Maumee in 1847. Charles Roby (who bought an interest in the ship) was celebrating his inaugural journey aboard the *Griffith* with his wife, children and several relatives. It carried 326 passengers: 256 in steerage, 45 in the cabin and a crew of 25, including many European immigrants headed west.

In the predawn hours of June 17, 1850, while hundreds of people slept on the ship, nothing unusual was noted during stops in Erie, Pennsylvania, and Fairport (its last stop before Cleveland), where it picked up more than a dozen additional passengers. Around 4:00 a.m., several people in Willoughby (present-day Willowick) saw a strange light on Lake Erie. It was the glow of a fire that would quickly engulf the *G.P. Griffith*.

Lakefront Lodge park. *Photo by M. Joanne Boresz.*

G.P. Griffith engraving, 1850. *Courtesy of Historical Collections of the Great Lakes, Bowling Green State University.*

The ship's first engineer, builder and designer, David R. Stebbins, was attending to the engine that morning. He had recently oiled the engine and reinforced the ship with the latest in fire prevention technologies.

"I did not discover the fire until the 2d. Mate gave the alarm," Stebbins said. "I then discovered the fire to be under the deck, by looking through two auger holes. It then appeared to be one sheet of fire on the under side. We got the hose in operation in less than three minutes. It did not seem more than ten minutes before the fire drove the away [*sic*]. I am part owner in the boat and believe that she was well secured from fire. I can hardly imagine how she took fire; but it is my impression that the fire caught at or near the bulkhead, near the freight hold."

Although he said lifeboats were prepared to launch, they weren't let down while the ship was moving for fear they would be swamped. By the time the ship slowed, the fire had rapidly spread, and the boats couldn't be reached.

In Roby's attempt to run the ship aground, it got stuck on a sandbar half a mile away from shore, within sight of today's Lakefront Lodge park. (Depending on wind direction and water level, some say the sandbar can still be seen.)

The verdict of the coroner's jury in the *Cleveland True Democrat* on June 18, 1850, stated:

> *It seems that while the boat was running, her motion drew the flames toward the stern, but as soon as she struck, the breeze from the lake took effect, and forced the flames forward, to where the passengers were assembled, with such rapidity that they were forced almost at the same instant to make the leap. The consequence was that the good swimmers were carried down and drowned by those who could not swim. It would seem as tho' they had sunk as one solid mass in one general embrace, and that too in only eight or nine feet of water.*

A survivor who gripped a wooden plank saw Captain Roby throw his mother, wife, daughter, infant son and the wife of the ship's barber into the lake in an attempt to save them. He then jumped into the water and sank with his wife in his arms. Roby's entire family died that day, but the barber's wife, known only as Price, was the only known woman to survive the disaster.

According to the coroner's report, by ten o'clock that morning, search parties had brought up 150 bodies. "The lake was so smooth and clear that we could see bodies as they lay upon the bottom, and so closely had they jumped in upon each other that when in one instance, one body was hooked and raised, eight others followed, holding fast to each other."

Since the ship's records were destroyed in the fire, the exact number of passengers is unknown, but it's estimated that 286 people died. Many people simply didn't know how to swim, while others might have been weighed down by their valuables, gold in their pockets or sewn into their clothes.

Only thirty-seven survivors were accounted for, and most owe their lives to Stebbins. According to passengers, he stood by his post on the *Griffith* until the very last moment. When it struck the sandbar, he immediately jumped in, swam to shore and was the first to reach land. Described as a man with great physical vigor, he managed to find a small skiff boat on the beach that he instantly launched back into the water toward the burning wreck and brought back three loads of passengers. One passenger, E.C. Holley, was reunited with his money belt, containing $2,300, and even found his hat, boots and trunk on shore.

Gold pocket watches, rings and jewelry were found on some of the deceased, along with paper money. It is possible that passengers' gold sank to the bottom of the lake during their struggle to survive after jumping from the *Griffith* and was covered by sand overtime, but it's also possible that this part of the story is purely legend.

Of the hundreds of bodies recovered, only one, the mother of Johnny Rhodes, had money tucked into the lining of her clothing. Captain Ransom Kennedy, who lived nearby (and started Willoughby Hardware Company in downtown Willoughby), saw Johnny lying on the beach. At first, he thought the child was dead but then noticed his lip quivering, so he quickly picked the boy up by his ankles and shook him until he coughed up water. Kennedy brought him back to his home to recover.

Johnny told Kennedy that his mother had $500 sewn into her petticoats, and news of this discovery brought thieves to the site a day later, greedily raiding graves for valuables.

Although Kennedy's family cared for Johnny following the shipwreck, Samuel Miller's family raised him to adulthood. Kennedy was said to have saved the money found in Johnny's mother's clothes to give to him, with interest, when he turned twenty-one, but unfortunately, Johnny died when he was nineteen while serving in the Civil War. He's buried in the cemetery, and a J.R. Miller (Johnny Rhodes Miller) is listed on the Civil War monument in Wes Point Park in downtown Willoughby.

A group of prominent residents quickly formed a committee to identify bodies that washed ashore. They decided, factoring in the summer heat, to immediately bury unidentified bodies in several long trenches dug farther back on the beach. About forty-seven men, twenty-four women and twenty-five children were in the first group buried in a mass grave, and a preacher came to pray for the lost souls. Although many accounts say the graves were located on the beach away from the water, others say the bodies were buried on a nearby bluff. The identified bodies were sent to Cleveland or were taken by family members, who provided proper burials.

Shortly after the disaster, theories began popping up about the cause of the fire. According to an article in the *Detroit Tribune*, the water tanks around the pipes where they pass through the decks were dry because the water was removed ten days earlier. Later studies found the "fire resistant" oil that Stebbins applied was in fact very flammable and explosive with a very low flash point. Another explanation was that paint stored too close to the firebox had overheated and had burst into flames. Yet one more source says that the *Griffith* was illegally carrying matches and/or turpentine that ignited. No matter what the cause, the results were catastrophic.

Several weeks after the fire, tragedy struck the *Griffith* again. According to an article in the Cleveland *Plain Dealer* on July 8, 1850, several scows, flat-bottomed boats, were sent to raise the *Griffith*.

G.P. Griffith Ohio Historical Marker at Lakefront Lodge, Willowick. *Photo by M. Joanne Boresz.*

A violent squall blew over the lake, and the scows capsized from the wind and waves. Nine men and a boy were saved by clinging to the rigging of the wreck, but Fairport resident Wallace Ames drowned—one more victim of the *Griffith* tragedy. There are varying reports about whether the bulk of the *Griffith*'s remains were eventually tugged ashore, but we do know that remnants are scattered across the bottom of Lake Erie in twenty to thirty feet of water. Over the years, divers have explored the wreck, and the engine, paddle wheel and bell were salvaged. Some say timbers and machinery are still visible.

The *Griffith* tragedy is the third-worst disaster on the Great Lakes, but it made navigation safer by bringing about important changes in the laws governing vessels on American waterways, which no doubt resulted in saving countless lives. Two years after the tragedy, the Steamboat Act of 1852 formed the base of today's Coast Guard marine safety program by improving the laws governing marine inspection.

In 2000, 150 years after the *Griffith* sank, an Ohio Historical Marker was placed at the top of the hill at Lakefront Lodge. It remains, facing out over the water where the *Griffith* met its fiery end, ensuring the lives lost that day will never be forgotten.

WILLOUGHBEACH AMUSEMENT PARK

More than one hundred years ago, men and women strolled along Lake Erie's shore in Lake County dressed in their finest clothes or the long, heavy bathing suits of the time. They were drawn to the serenity of the water's edge just as we are today. They flocked in droves to parks and summer resorts like Linden Beach on the Painesville-Fairport border and Salida Beach in Mentor-on-the-Lake, but Willoughbeach Amusement Park, in present-day Willowick, was the crown jewel.

The property overlooking the lake, across from today's Shoregate Shopping Center, began with cottages, bathing areas and dance pavilions and was transformed into an amusement park by 1898. It was developed and owned by Cleveland, Painesville & Eastern (CP&E) interurban railway owners Henry Everett and Edward Moore, and the interurban rail line stop they added to the entrance of their property helped ensure its success.

For several decades in the late 1800s to early 1900s, Willowick was known by two names: Village of Willoughbeach and Willoughby-on-the-Lake (later

Postcard showing entrance to Willoughbeach Amusement Park. *Courtesy of Linda Zinn.*

becoming Willowick when the Willo from Willoughby was combined with the Wick from Wickliffe).

By the early 1900s Willougbeach was thriving, with area churches and businesses holding annual picnics on the grounds. There were campgrounds and baseball fields and stands for Willoughbeach baseball games. There were rides, including a carousel and an innovative, yet likely highly hazardous, auto roller coaster known as the Jack Rabbit. It allowed car owners to drive their cars up a steep track and coast down the ravine on a narrow wooden track. Hydroplanes were even known to land at Willoughbeach, as shown in several pictures from the early 1900s.

Visitors from Cleveland escaped to the lakeside retreat by paying just twenty-five cents per round-trip ticket on the interurban line, which transported up to five hundred visitors. For many years, Willoughbeach was a very lucrative business for Moore and Everett as they collected both railway fares and admission to the park.

There was, however, a dark side to the amusement park. The site is said to have spanned the area where victims of the *Griffith* disaster were buried on a bluff set back from the lake and not on the sand, as some sources had insisted. There is an account of a man, who wished to remain anonymous, who ran the carousel at Willoughbeach Amusement Park. He worked hard to keep it shiny and clean each day but was also assigned the gruesome

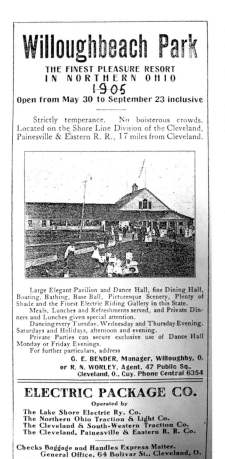

Willoughbeach Park

THE FINEST PLEASURE RESORT
IN NORTHERN OHIO
1905
Open from May 30 to September 23 inclusive

Strictly temperance. No boisterous crowds. Located on the Shore Line Division of the Cleveland, Painesville & Eastern R. R., 17 miles from Cleveland.

Large Elegant Pavilion and Dance Hall, fine Dining Hall, Boating, Bathing, Base Ball, Picturesque Scenery, Plenty of Shade and the Finest Electric Riding Gallery in this State.
Meals, Lunches and Refreshments served, and Private Dinners and Lunches given special attention.
Dancing every Tuesday, Wednesday and Thursday Evening. Saturdays and Holidays, afternoon and evening.
Private Parties can secure exclusive use of Dance Hall Monday or Friday Evenings.
For further particulars, address
G. E. BENDER, Manager, Willoughby, O.
or **R. N. WORLEY, Agent, 47 Public Sq.,**
Cleveland, O., Cuy. Phone Central 6354

ELECTRIC PACKAGE CO.
Operated by
The Lake Shore Electric Ry. Co.
The Northern Ohio Traction & Light Co.
The Cleveland & South-Western Traction Co.
The Cleveland, Painesville & Eastern R. R. Co.

Checks Baggage and Handles Express Matter.
General Office, 64 Bolivar St., Cleveland, O.

Willoughbeach advertisement, 1905.
Courtesy of Willoughby Historical Society.

task of checking in the nearby soil for bones that regularly eroded and then disposing of them.

The rise of the automobile and development of other amusement parks along the lake, like Euclid Beach and Cedar Point to the west and Geauga Lake to the east, eventually took a toll on the once-thriving park. The amusement park officially closed in May 1926, but the site stayed open, allowing visitors access to the beach and campgrounds into the late 1930s.

Today, remnants of the park remain on Cresthaven Drive, across from Shoregate and just east of Willowick City Hall and the new Larimar home development. A simple wooden green sign, stating, "Willo Beach Park," stands over a path between several trees, marking the entrance of the gated private neighborhood park founded in 1945.

On a hot summer day in 2019, club member Tim Hanson graciously allowed my family and me to wander the park I had once played at as a kid, looking for signs of the old amusement park. The wooden pavilion on the lower end of the park, near the edge of a bluff overlooking Lake Erie, had white paint peeling away on the underside of the roof, exposing worn wood and perhaps decades of history.

Long-time members Charlie and Barbara McMahon were there enjoying the beautiful view of the lake. Charlie is president and Barbara is secretary of the Willo-Beach Park Association board. They believe the pavilion is one of the original amusement park pavilions that are seen in several old photographs. Where a stretch of beach once existed below, water now crashes against a cliff lined with leaning trees and exposed roots. However, the size, square shape and triangular roof of the pavilion all match up

Perfection Spring Company Outing, August 11, 1917. In front of car coaster at Willoughbeach Amusement Park. *Courtesy of Willoughby Historical Society. Restoration by Ron Kotar, Studio K Photography.*

Willoughbeach baseball team. *Courtesy of Willoughby Historical Society.*

Pavilion at Willo Beach neighborhood beach park. *Photo by author.*

Postcard showing beach and pavilions at Willoughbeach Amusement Park. *Courtesy of Willoughby Historical Society.*

with the one in the black-and-white photos. The only difference is the four corners that are now square pillars.

Barbara believes the original round wooden tree pillars remain underneath and were "wrapped" with the flat pieces of wood in the 1970s to give it a modern look. The smaller beams, which look like small tree trunks, extending from the pillars to the top of the roof can still be seen and perfectly match the ones in the photographs. Due to lake erosion, there is no way to tell if this pavilion is in its original place. Perhaps several buildings were reclaimed by the lake and members at one time decided to move it back to preserve it for the future.

Besides some old bricks found strewn about in the middle of a wooded area in the park, old-looking light fixtures and a small sewer grate covered by grass that might be from the days of the amusement park, this is the only remaining visible remnant of Willoughbeach Amusement Park.

FAIRPORT HARBOR LIGHTHOUSE

In 1807, Samuel Huntington (nephew of a signer of the Declaration of Independence) arrived on the Western Reserve from Connecticut. After several years in Cleveland, he decided he didn't like the climate and wanted to find a new home, so he exchanged properties with Cleveland's postmaster and collector of the port, John Walworth, to be closer to his job, and Huntington gained two thousand acres of land by the Grand River.

Huntington, who quickly became involved in community affairs, wanted to provide the area with a port, so in 1812, along with Abraham Skinner, he laid out the town of Grandon, named after its location at the mouth of the Grand River. Grandon became a thriving port and village, and its name changed to Fairport when it was incorporated, with *Harbor* added later.

In 1818, steamboats began to be used on Lake Erie, with the pioneering sidewheel steamboat *Walk in the Water.* Fairport was its third trip, bringing ten people ashore.

A need for a lighthouse became obvious, and in 1825, proposals for such a structure appeared in two March editions of the *Painesville Telegraph.* Jonathan Goldsmith and Hiram Wood were contracted to build a stone or brick whitewashed tower and a two-story keeper's dwelling on Lake Erie at the mouth of the Grand River.

According to one of Goldsmith's daughters, while the lighthouse was being constructed, he drove in a wagon to Erie to get a rope and tackle to hoist the lantern to the top of the tower. She said it was the longest rope she had ever seen, and it filled the entire back of the wagon.

By the fall of 1825, the fifty-five-foot-tall lighthouse was completed, at a cost of $5,032, with a fixed white light fueled by whale oil. It was the third lighthouse built on Lake Erie by the U.S. government, preceded only by lighthouses in Erie, Pennsylvania, and Sandusky Bay.

Thanks in part to the lighthouse, Fairport soon became known as a "sailor's town," rivaling the port of Cleveland. In fact, by the mid-1800s, it was the second-largest port on Lake Erie, with three thousand ships and $1 million in annual business. It also became a final stop on the Underground Railroad, thanks to the townspeople ensuring its flashing light stood as a beacon of freedom for escaped enslaved people who were often hidden in the lighthouse and smuggled onto Canada-bound ships.

Years after building the lighthouse, in 1841, Goldsmith applied for an open position to be the keeper of the Fairport light, but even with Congressman Joshua Giddings championing his cause, he was not selected.

After only a decade, the lighthouse began to have major structural issues, yet it still served the Lake Erie coastline forty-four years, thanks to regular maintenance and repairs. It was eventually demolished, and on March 3,

Postcard of Fairport Harbor Lighthouse. *Authors collection.*

1869, Congress allotted $30,000 to rebuild the Fairport Harbor Light House on the same footprint as the original. By August 11, 1871, the tower was completed, and the light shone once again, with the original Fresnel light transferred to the new structure. The tower was sixteen feet wide at the base, with sixty-nine steps winding up to the top, and by that October, the keeper's dwelling was also rebuilt. The light guided ships in the harbor for one hundred years, from 1825 to 1925, and had fourteen different keepers throughout its history. This lighthouse still stands today and houses the Fairport Harbor Marine Museum.

LIVING IN THE FAIRPORT HARBOR WEST BREAKWATER LIGHTHOUSE

On the east end of an expanse of beach at Mentor Headlands State Park (the largest natural beach in the state) stands a striking square-shaped white lighthouse with a red roof. The Fairport Harbor West Breakwater Lighthouse sits between the area's two largest public beaches—Headlands and Fairport Harbor.

Without a tenant for many years, it fell into disrepair, but in 2009, when Shelia Consaul learned the federal government was auctioning off old lighthouses that no longer needed to house Coast Guard personnel, she decided it would be a perfect summer home away from the hustle and bustle of Washington, D.C. Although she was outbid several times, the other bidders defaulted, and she was finally able to get her dream home in 2011.

"Thus began my love affair with Northeast Ohio, Lake County, Fairport Harbor, and my quest to restore the property to its original grandeur and create for myself the 'ultimate' summer home," Consaul said.

Consaul's lease agreement gives the Coast Guard access when needed to the beacon on top of the lighthouse, now run by a large solar panel on the platform, since it is still an active aid to navigation for mariners on Lake Erie. It also houses a National Weather Service station, tracking weather conditions for both beachgoers and researchers.

She says many people ask about the original Fresnel mechanism that lit the harbor when the lighthouse was first lit on June 9, 1925, but she unfortunately doesn't know what happened to it. "It would be nice to think that the Coast Guard replaced it at some point and has it neatly packed away in storage. However, I haven't been able to find out if that is true."

Fairport Harbor West Breakwater Lighthouse. *Photo by Brenda Traffis.*

The lighthouse is five stories from the basement up to the lantern room, with a circular staircase connecting each floor. She says renovating her home has been one of the biggest challenges of living in a lighthouse. "There are only two ways to access the structure: 1) parking in Mentor Headlands State Park and walking through the beach area, along the steep rock break wall, and scaling the platform with the help of an extension ladder 2) taking a boat to the east side of the platform where there is a set of stairs cut into the side, disembarking from the boat there, and climbing the uneven steps to the top of the platform."

While walking the break wall isn't particularly easy, Consaul has managed to haul some loads of provisions that way, with her backpack full of gasoline for her generator, cans of paint and brushes and water and household goods. She's even carried the lighthouse's cake for the annual public Birthday Open House held each June.

When she wanders through her unique home, she can't help but think of the men who lived in and cared for the lighthouse decades ago, like Daniel Babcock, the first lighthouse keeper, who served from 1925 to 1936. He was

Young woman named Jen Mackey sitting on Fairport Harbor break wall, early 1920s. *Photo by Sheldon Joseph Harris, courtesy of his granddaughter Katherine Harris Szerdy.*

also the last lighthouse keeper of the Grand River Lighthouse at Fairport, having taken over for his father, Joseph, before it was decommissioned in 1919.

Frank LaRosa served as a keeper for a decade, starting in 1927, and created some important service standards, like arranging watches so that two of the three men assigned to the station were always at the lighthouse, along with creating an emergency signal to summon help from shore.

John Brophy was the last head keeper in 1937, after spending five years in charge of the Ashtabula Lighthouse. After that, the lighthouse's history becomes sketchy, but Consaul knows an empty building was left behind in 1948, when the last keeper moved out, and it remained empty for many years. During that time, it was left vulnerable to looters and trespassers, and it was stripped and vandalized, leaving behind very few items of historical relevance.

Some of the most interesting aspects of the lighthouse are in the service room, like a smaller staircase leading to the lantern room, where a door opens to the outside widow's walk. There's also a large iron trapdoor in the service room that is hinged from the top. Consaul says it takes up a good portion of the north side, and she isn't sure what its exact purpose was but suspects it might have been used to bring in the original fourth order Fresnel light from below the service room before hoisting it into place in the lantern room.

She did find a few treasures tucked in the attic and stashed in the basement, including ten fully intact glass panels that were used as interior storm windows, along with a solid iron ladder that was propped up in the basement to access a room that served as the original cistern. She discovered an old foghorn that now makes the perfect end table. She says she found an interesting artifact in the lighthouse eaves, accessed by squeezing through a thirty-six-by-thirty-six square opening. It's a large wooden shipping crate with a small paper delivery label on the front with the shipping address Fairport Harbor West Breakwater Light Station. According to the large painted lettering, the crate contained a Frigidaire refrigerator, shipped from Dayton on April 27, 1947, taking one full month to travel from one corner of the state to the other. Although, there's no evidence of the actual refrigerator in the lighthouse, she says as she continues her renovation, there is no telling what other interesting artifacts she might uncover.

"Who's to say there isn't some long-lost pirate booty, European jewels or a missing copy of the Declaration of Independence? Don't worry, I'll keep looking."

ADVENTURER ROBERT MANRY

On any given day in the summer, Manry Park, on Arnold Road in Willowick, is full of activity. Kids climb on the playground, swim in the pool or play baseball on the fields. "I'll meet you at Manry," is often uttered by residents; however, many don't realize that the park was named after a great adventurer who made a solo journey across the Atlantic Ocean in a thirteen-and-a-half-foot sailboat.

Robert Manry. *Courtesy of Special Collections, Cleveland State University Library.*

For years, Willowick resident Robert "Bob" Manry worked the night shift as a copy editor at the *Plain Dealer*, dreaming of getting away from "the sedentary life of the copy desk" and setting sail across the sea. Although shy, he was known for his ready smile and distinctive booming laugh.

Manry eventually bought a small boat from a family in Cleveland for just thirty dollars. Little did that family know that he would completely overhaul it, adding a new mast and sleeping quarters, and would eventually make history in it.

The Manry family, including Bob's wife, Virginia, and children, Robin and Douglas, named the boat *Tinkerbelle* after the kids' fascination with *Peter Pan*. They added the *e* like the French word *belle*, meaning beautiful.

He planned his voyage for fourteen months, even teaching himself celestial navigation. He tucked enormous stashes of provisions into his tiny cabin before leaving Willowick for Falmouth, Massachusetts, with Virginia on May 23, 1965, pulling *Tinkerbelle* with his station wagon.

Manry's goal was to reach another town named Falmouth across the Atlantic in Cornwall, England. Many people thought it was a crazy and dangerous proposal, but Manry was determined.

"*Tinkerbelle* already had taken six-foot waves and about thirty-knot winds on Lake Erie without having to heave to and I was confident that, hove, she could survive conditions that were far more severe," wrote Manry in the book he wrote about his experience, *Tinkerbelle*.

His voyage began on June 1, 1965, and was slow-moving, with a top speed of just seven knots and an average that was much lower. He said he went about forty miles a day and often had cloudy weather that made navigation difficult.

Being alone for so long was also challenging, but the captains of large boats stopped him several times to make sure he was OK, since he was in such a small sailboat out in the middle of the sea. When he was one hundred miles away from Falmouth, the captain of a Belgian ship insisted on giving Manry a whole roast turkey, potato croquettes and a few bottles of beer and 7UP. He said it was like Thanksgiving.

Manry also had a few visits from his wife, Virginia, as he got closer to England. It was a welcome respite from a grueling journey that had knocked him into the sea six times (although he quickly got back in his boat because he was afraid of sharks).

His plans on reaching the shore were to "kiss the old Mother Earth and next thing is to take a bath."

He was becoming an international media sensation, and since the trip was taking longer than it was initially expected, people began to worry. However, Virginia was confident in his sailing abilities and said anyone who knew him wouldn't be concerned. She said she and Bob wouldn't even take *Tinkerbelle* out on Lake Erie unless there was a small craft advisory because they needed the wind and waves to get it moving. According to Bob, his trip was taking longer because a current took him north to Ireland, which he didn't realize right away because of cloud coverage, but he quickly rerouted himself back toward England.

After seventy-eight days at sea, he was thrust into the spotlight when he approached Falmouth on August 17, 1965. Boatloads of people were surrounding his small sailboat as he inched toward shore, paying a pound a piece to board crowded ships just to see him. Another fifty thousand people were waiting on shore, clapping and cheering. It was described as absolute chaos.

When Manry finally climbed off his boat onto land with shaky legs, media cameras were watching. He kissed his wife and kids and then kissed the ground.

In the documentary about his journey, *Manry at Sea: In the Wake of a Dream*, Manry said he was "flabbergasted" by the huge crowds of people pushing and shoving to see him and even trying to touch his car as he drove away. Some people said it was like the rock band The Beatles were going through. It was just the beginning of Manry mania.

When asked why he took such a dangerous journey with a wife and two children at home (Robin was thirteen and Douglas was ten), he replied, "There comes a time when you must choose to either risk everything to achieve your dreams or spend the rest of your life in your own backyard."

Robert Manry arriving in Falmouth on *Tinkerbelle*, August 17, 1965. *Courtesy of Special Collections, Cleveland State University Library.*

The Manry family returned to the United States on the *Queen Mary* ocean liner, and Bob appeared on a number of shows including the *Tonight Show*, *Today Show* and *What's My Line?*

On arrival in Cleveland, Manry was met by local dignitaries and received a key to the city. He was welcomed home to Willowick with a parade and ten thousand people cheering for him, and he was escorted to his home on Royalview Drive by a police car, with friends, family and residents lining his driveway. Along with having a park named after him, Manry received a number of gifts when he returned, like a Honda motorcycle, two paintings of himself in *Tinkerbelle*, a plaque from the city and an honorary membership in the Willowick Kiwanis Club.

Bob never returned to the copy desk and instead became a successful writer and speaker. In 1966, he published *Tinkerbelle* about his voyage, and it became an international best seller.

In 1967, he bought a twenty-seven-foot Tartan that the Manry family named *Curlew* to take them on a yearlong adventure around the eastern half of the United States. He also donated *Tinkerbelle* to the Western Reserve Historical Society in Cleveland, where it remains today in its Crawford Auto-Aviation Museum.

Robert and Virginia Manry aboard *Curlew* at Mentor Harbor Yacht Club, 1967. *Courtesy of Special Collections, Cleveland State University Library.*

He began writing another book about this second journey when they returned home, but on May 2, 1969, Virginia died in a one-car crash on the Ohio Turnpike after visiting her very ill mother in Pittsburgh.

Manry was so shattered that it is said he never sailed again and was unable to continue writing his second book. In October 1970, Bob married Jean Flaherty, of Pittsburgh, but he died of a heart attack at the age of fifty-two while they were visiting friends in Union City, Pennsylvania, on February 21, 1971.

Today, Manry's kids live in Cleveland. Their childhood home on Royalview Drive in Willowick, where *Tinkerbelle* got its start, is privately owned.

Manry Park Nike Site

Manry Park wasn't always just a place for locals to socialize and play sports. Before it was named after Robert Manry, it was actually a government-run site during the Cold War years, when the United States was under the threat of a nuclear attack.

Several years after President Harry Truman approved the Federal Civil Defense Act of 1950, "designed to protect life and property in the United States in case of enemy assault," Nike Missile bases were built throughout northeast Ohio to counter an airborne threat from the Soviet Union. There were seven sites in Cuyahoga County and one in Lake County. In Eastlake, there was a launch base at 33605 Curtis Boulevard, with its control area based at present-day Manry. Each launch base held a battery of Nike-Ajax missiles, missile-assembly, generators, acid-storage buildings, underground missile storage and launchers, a fueling area, barracks and a launcher-control trailer. The control areas were placed half a mile from the launch site. Although Manry Park didn't house any silos for missiles, from 1957 to 1962, it provided living quarters ready to be used by several army battalions, along with a mess hall and radar center.

The Federal Civil Defense Agency (FDCA), authorized under the Federal Civil Defense Act, educated the public about the new national program and prepared them for the possibility of a nuclear attack, teaching citizens to organize local operations to protect themselves and their communities. Because civil defense received very little government funding, finding volunteers became imperative.

My dad, ham operator Dale Boresz, was one of those volunteers, since he had the ability, if needed, to help communicate from the site. He thankfully

Manry Park. *Photo by Summer DeMore Boresz.*

never had to take on that role, but he recalls driving in a few parades as a Civil Defense volunteer.

These Nike sites were relatively short-lived and were closed or demolished by the early '70s. When the Nike site closed at present-day Manry, Willoughby-Eastlake Board of Education bought it and used the rooms inside the buildings for kindergarten classes. In 1964, as Manry was readying for his voyage overseas, the City of Willowick purchased the site for $66,650 and turned the buildings and surrounding area into storage and recreational use.

3

Unique Structures

Hilo Farm

Hilo Farm is a sprawling English Tudor–style complex at the corner of Little Mountain and Hart Roads. The Kirtland Hills estate contains a number of buildings, including the oldest home in Ohio, dating to 1472.

It was the summer home of Leonard C. Hanna Jr., heir to the Hanna mining fortune, from 1924 until 1957. He grew up on Cleveland's Millionaires' Row, with neighbors including the Gilded Age elite. He attended Yale in 1909, where he met Cole Porter (soon to be famous composer and songwriter).

After graduating and living in New York City, Hanna came back to Ohio and bought 316 acres of land in Kirtland Hills. He hired architects Derrick & Gamber to build a country estate replicating a fifteenth-century English Tudor village and named it HiLo Farm after his favorite card game, High-Low Jack. The land, first settled in 1814 by Levi Smith, was a fully working farm with horses, cows, ducks and sheep; a kennel for Leonard's Weimaraner dogs; a greenhouse; a pool; tennis courts; and the only covered bridge in Lake County, which remains on the property to this day.

The main house was constructed around the smaller historic English Tudor manor. Department store magnate John Wanamaker first bought the home, had it disassembled and shipped it to the United States. Then Cleveland industrialist Edmund Burke had it rebuilt as his guest house on his Hunting Valley estate. To save it from demolition, Hanna moved it to Hilo Farm in 1945 and added two wings.

Hilo Farm gatehouse. *Courtesy of private collection.*

Hanna entertained famous friends at his estate, including Cole Porter, Humphrey Bogart, Joan Crawford, Lauren Bacall and Eleanor Roosevelt. According to legend, Gloria Swanson once lost an earring in his pool. It was believed that the dog ate it, and it was discovered later in his dog pen. Other accounts say the earring actually belonged to comedienne Phyllis Diller.

Locals often parked along Hart Road to listen to the sounds of Cole Porter on piano wafting from inside Hilo Farm. Leonard and his self-titled "Jolly Gang" passed the summer months in luxury, but he didn't keep all of his wealth to himself. When he was fifty-two years old and retired, he headed to England at the start of World War II, where he set up one hundred canteens for U.S. troops. He planned to open more but became ill and returned home.

In northeast Ohio, Leonard Hanna's name is synonymous with giving. He was a generous theater patron, donated to University Hospital and gave $150,000 to match Mentor mayor Eleanor Garfield's fund to build Garfield Park. He was a lifelong art collector and donated his collection to the Cleveland Museum of Art. He helped fund the new wing in 1956, and when he died a year later, at just sixty-seven years old, his will provided an endowment that transformed the museum's collection.

In 1957, part of the Hanna estate was subdivided, and modern homes were built, but the beautiful, nearly century old main buildings of Hilo Farm remain and are privately owned.

Hilo Farm buildings, including dovecote on left and gatehouse on right with old Elm tree at end. *Photo by author.*

The current owners of the gatehouse and working farm portion of Hanna's estate have been committed to preserving their historic property since they moved in more than two decades ago. They say Hanna, being in the shipping industry, actually built a railroad from Lake Erie to Hilo to bring in the materials to build his estate. There's even an English garden on the property, built when Hanna was out of town. According to the owners, when he returned and saw the garden, he hated it and refused to ever go in. Their property includes the gatehouse with maids' quarters, a milking parlor and creamery and a garage, along with outlying buildings, like a sheep house, chicken house (renovated to be a pool house), smoke house, corn crib and dovecote (currently attracting bats instead of doves). One of the largest trees in Ohio that survived the Dutch Elm Disease also stands grandly on their property.

The owners graciously gave me a tour of their beautiful home, pointing out original pieces, like a small table and a set of four chairs covered in elephant hide, a sturdy barn door with original working hardware and an icebox now used as a pantry. They have worked meticulously to restore the

English gardens at Hilo Farm. *Photo by author.*

buildings by matching original windows, hardware and woodwork, while also modernizing the estate. Although they bring in outside contractors, they've done a lot of work themselves, hand-weathering and carving grooves into wood to restore ceilings and maintaining the lush rolling hills and vibrant flowers on their property by personally taking on roles of gardener and grass mower.

The family also has a historic treasure from Hilo Farm's earliest days that was left behind by a previous owner—a framed envelope from Cole Porter addressed to Leonard Hanna.

CONFECTIONARY CUPBOARD

While driving south on OH-615 in Mentor, you'll come across a beautiful brick building on the right-hand side that houses a bakery called the Confectionary Cupboard. It's filled with the comforting aromas of cake. A century ago, it likely contained an equally pleasing smell (for some people) of books and was originally located on the northeast corner of Mentor Avenue and Center Street.

The Mentor Library Company, formed in 1819, was the first library in Mentor and the first subscription library in the Western Reserve. It was created by thirty-six men from surrounding cities and townships, and it cost twenty-five-cents a year to borrow books, including *The Life of Washington* and John Bunyan's *The Holy War*.

In 1859, the last signature of a returned book was recorded, but no one knows what happened to the library's two hundred books after that. It's possible that the depression of 1857 impacted the library.

In 1889, James R. Garfield, son of President James A. Garfield, created a board to discuss building a new library, and his mother, Lucretia, hosted fundraising events and donated fifty dollars and books. This new library, located at Village Hall, opened in 1890 with 288 books that patrons could borrow for up to two weeks. There was a two-cent-per-day charge for overdue books and rules against talking loudly or using tobacco while visiting.

It hosted community events like lectures, spelling bees, melodramas and socials. A pound grab bag night was a popular, yet unusual, event in which partygoers brought a one-pound package wrapped in newspaper and took turns grabbing a bag. If their bag was full of food, they had to eat it on the spot, and if it had clothing inside, they had to wear it immediately.

A decade later, the library's books surpassed the area's population, which was about 1,800, and began outgrowing its space. The town raised $4,000 to build a new library on the northeast corner of Mentor Avenue and Center Street. Abram Garfield, James R.'s brother, drew up plans for a colonial-style building. Abram had his own architectural firm in Cleveland and had studied at Williams College and Massachusetts Institute of Technology. He

Above: Confectionary Cupboard in old Mentor Library building. *Photo by author.*

Opposite, top: Postcard from the old Mentor Library, between 1908 and 1922. *Courtesy of Pat Huebner.*

Opposite, bottom: Old Mentor Library moving to new location. *Photo by David Gartner.*

had designed many other well-known buildings, including several at Lake Erie College in Painesville, Wildwood in Mentor and Eldred Hall at Case Western Reserve University.

The $7,693 library opened in 1903, and three years later, Frances Estelle Cleveland became the first librarian. She worked hard to cultivate a love of reading among the children in the community and delivered books by horse and wagon to schools in the township. She was so dedicated that even on cold days in the unheated library, she worked after hours building bookshelves by hand. During the Great Depression, when the library board greatly reduced funding, Frances even worked for free for the first three months of the year so that the library could buy more books. For years, she continued to expand the library and promote literature, but in 1944, after a yearlong illness, she died, and the community mourned her loss.

After nearly five decades, the Mentor library, which was once grand in size, was too small to meet the demand of a growing community, so in

1960, a new library opened on Mentor Avenue. It could hold up to sixty-five thousand books.

The original library was at risk of being demolished, but Mentor realtor Lila Moore Schaefer understood its historical value and bought it, moving the entire building to her property on the corner of Nowlen and Center Streets, where it remains. For several years, it housed Lila's living quarters and real estate business, but in 1964, she died suddenly, and the building was repossessed. In 1979, it was placed on the National Register of Historic Places and has had several other owners.

More than a decade ago, Pat Huebner and her family bought the building to house their business—the Confectionary Cupboard. With a degree in interior design and love of old architecture she knew it was right for them from the very beginning. She says, unfortunately, not much is left of the building's original interior details. Frances's handmade bookshelves are long gone, but intricate detailing remains on the interior molding and columns. Only one of the two original fireplaces remains.

Huebner says people are surprised to learn there is a second floor (where the library's children's section once existed) and an attic. She's heard that previous tenants in the building thought it was haunted and claimed to see a rocking chair rock on its own on the second floor. Although she and the Confectionary Cupboard staff joke when something happens that "it must be Francis," she says the building has always had a warm, positive feeling. In fact, it continues in the tradition that it was created—bringing joy to people—at first through books and now through cake.

BRENNAN'S FISH HOUSE

Brennan's Fish House in the Village of Grand River was built alongside the Grand River in 1865 and has remained in business continuously since then. It has withstood hits to the economy during the Great Depression and wars, starting with the end of the Civil War when it was built. Customers have arrived by foot, horse, carriage and later automobile. In fact, its current parking lot, made of six parcels of land, was once dotted with small cottages housing the families of local fishermen.

The building was first built as a hotel, known as the Richmond Inn. In 1847, Grand River was named Richmond after Thomas Richmond, a salt merchant from New York who came to the area with dreams of making

Brennan's Fish House, Grand River. *Photo by Korene Engelking.*

it a busy canal town. More than three thousand ships in the ore and coal industry had arrived at the port that year, bringing in more than $1 million in commerce.

Although the region saw a boom for a while, business declined when Cleveland won the race to be the port of the Ohio and Erie Canal. The hotel never took off as the owners had hoped, so they decided to cater to the local clientele of sailors and fishermen by installing pool tables, selling beer and even running it as a brothel.

During this period, the area was very rough, with bars lining the riverfront. A notorious local character named Pearl was a saloonkeeper and opera singer who had been married five times. She was known for keeping a small knife in a belt around her dress and didn't tolerate funny business from her customers. If they were acting up, she tossed them out.

Then from 1927 to 1966, George and Martha Evans ran the building as a diner, raising their ten children in the living quarters upstairs. The Evanses dug a dirt-floor basement beneath the building, spanning half of the home from front to back, to store food like jars of fruit and canned vegetables.

Next it was run as a bar called Harry's, with owners Harry and Helen Jones living upstairs with their children.

Future owner Tim Brennan grew up nearby in Fairport. Although his father gave strict instructions that he and his nine siblings were not to swim across the river, Tim did so pretty regularly to get french fries from Harry's. In 1973, while working at Lincoln Electric, Tim and his wife, Betty, took a leap of faith and bought the building, changing its name to Brennan's Fish House. They expanded the original structure to add more dining space, but never lived upstairs.

Current owner Sharon Hill and her husband, Steve, bought the restaurant and all-important recipes that customers love from the Brennans in 2006 while she was working there as a hostess. They lived upstairs with the youngest two of their four children.

In 2016, Steve suddenly passed away. It was a devastating loss for Sharon, but she continued to make the restaurant a success with help and support from her children, friends, family and customers.

The customers have actually helped build the interior of Brennan's over the years. The walls are lined with pictures and memorabilia like captain's hats and boat fixtures that were donated by patrons. Sharon says they have century-old paintings of ships that were often commissioned by the ship's owners to hang proudly in their homes.

A life ring hanging above a restaurant window always fascinated Sharon. She never understood what the words on it meant, since they were in a foreign language, until several years after buying the restaurant. One day, an older gentleman eating at the restaurant told her, "That life ring belonged to me. It was on my boat." It turns out the life ring he had given to the Brennans years ago has a special story behind it.

The man had fought in Vietnam on a swift boat, going up and down the delta. He painted *Zin Loi* on his swift boat, meaning "tough ship" in Vietnamese. It was a dangerous act with a powerful statement. At the time, he said if he ever got home alive, he would buy a boat and name it Zin Loi. He did just that, and after enjoying it for some time decided to sell the boat, but he kept the life ring as a memento.

A lot has changed in the building over the years as renovations have taken place, but some things remain, like the original wooden liquor shelves that are still in use. Although it's a lot of work maintaining an old building like this, Sharon says it's worth preserving. "I think that what kept it going for many, many years was the fact that the people that owned it lived here and breathed here," Sharon said. "It was everyone's entire life, as well as ours. The owners were always present and that makes a big difference."

THE MATCHWORKS BUILDING

The Matchworks Building at 8500 Station Street is a stately example of reinvention. The fifty-thousand-square-foot brick building sits alongside the railroad tracks and is a focal point on the city skyline, with a tall tower that can be seen while driving down Route 615. It's a reminder of the various industries that were once pivotal to the bustling city of Mentor.

The Matchworks Building was actually Mentor's first industrial building. It was built in 1868 for $11,500 and started as Hart Nut and Washer Company, a nut and bolt factory. When an inventor came up with an even better product, Hart Nut and Washer Company was eventually forced to close.

Over the years, it changed hands again and again, first as a short-lived flouring mill and then as Mentor Knitting Mills Company, established in 1891 after more land was purchased and extensive additions were made. First-class machinery was installed, and more than 150 people worked at the plant. The company was known for its "Mentor comfort underwear," which were advertised and sold in every state. The mills did very well while the owners were alive, but when management changed, the plant began to decline and was never able to recover.

Postcard of Mentor "business section," early 1900s. *Courtesy of Greg Eyler.*

Postcard of Mentor Knitting Mills, 1913. *Author's collection.*

After everything was dismantled and sold, the Lake Shore Chemical Company operated out of the building from 1916 to 1917, producing an ingredient used to make poisonous gas for World War I. It was followed by the Salvet Company, which made animal tonics, and then the Ames Bag Company, which made cloth bags used for salt, in 1923.

In 1938, the Columbia Match Company was founded by James H. Weaver and his two sons, and it became the buildings most successful business to date. The company produced matchbooks and match-making machines for an international market. It's also where the Matchworks building derived its modern name.

In 1955, it was purchased by the Production Machinery Corporation. When it closed, the building underwent yet another major renovation, and in the '80s, commercial office spaces were created, which have been filled since then with both restaurants and businesses.

JAMES A. GARFIELD NATIONAL HISTORIC SITE

The James A. Garfield National Historic Site on Mentor Avenue was the home of our nation's twentieth president. Garfield lived at Lawnfield, named by the press during his 1880 presidential campaign, with his wife, Lucretia "Crete" Rudolph, and five children, Harry, James R., Molly, Irvin and Abram. They also had two children who died very young, Eliza and Edward.

Garfield, born in 1831 in Orange Township, was the last president born in a log cabin. He was raised in poverty but excelled at school and graduated from Williams College in Massachusetts. He returned to northeast Ohio to teach at Western Reserve Eclectic Institute (later Hiram College), where he met Lucretia.

Garfield enlisted as a Union soldier in the Civil War, eventually becoming brigadier general. Although elected to the U.S. House of Representatives in 1862, he stayed with his troops until 1863, when he left to take his elected seat. The well-liked and respected congressman helped pass the Thirteenth Amendment, ending slavery, and the Fourteenth and Fifteenth Amendments, providing for full citizenship and equal protection under the law for formerly enslaved people and voting rights for Black men. By 1876, he had settled down in Lake County, buying a 118-acre farm in the rural village of Mentor. Several years later, he raised the roof of his one-and-a-half-story home and expanded its outer walls, doubling its size.

In 1880, Garfield intended to support John Sherman for the presidential nomination at the Chicago convention but ended up being nominated after someone shouted, "We want Garfield," and others clearly agreed.

After he returned to the farm, crowds gathered on his front lawn to hear the leader with a commanding presence and tall stature give patriotic speeches in his deep baritone voice. People began arriving by train (a platform was built at the stop to support the influx) and walking a mile and a half through fields to reach Garfield's front porch. Since candidates didn't campaign at the time, this became our nation's first front porch presidential campaign.

He was the first president to give a speech in a foreign language (speaking German to immigrants) and spoke six languages, including French, Greek, Latin and Hebrew, the latter because he wanted to read the Bible in its original language. He was said to be ambidextrous, writing in two different languages with different hands at the same time.

According to volunteers at the James A. Garfield National Historic Site, during one of the speeches, Garfield's son had a little fun and stood in the back of the gathered crowd, yelling out, "Hurrah for Hancock!" (Democrat Winfield S. Hancock was Garfield's opponent.) There is no official word on whether Garfield found this amusing or infuriating.

Left: President James A. Garfield. *Courtesy of Library of Congress.*

Right: Garfield's campaign office at Lawnfield. *Photo by author.*

Garfield turned his personal library, a small building behind his house, into a campaign office, complete with wired-in telegraph. On November 2, 1880, about twenty family members and friends gathered at the Garfield home, eagerly awaiting the election results. Forty-nine-year-old Garfield was in his office, and his children excitedly ran back and forth sharing the latest updates with everyone in the house. At midnight, Lawnfield erupted in celebration as Garfield triumphed, and everyone gathered in the dining room to enjoy a feast of ham in champagne sauce, duck and oysters. As of this writing, Garfield's margin of victory is the narrowest among presidents who won the popular vote.

After heading to the White House, Garfield planned to focus his attention on civil rights, education and economic growth, but just several months into his term, his wife became very sick with malaria. When she was on the mend, the Garfields decided that a vacation would be good for everyone's health, but on July 2, 1881, when Garfield was preparing to board a train at the Baltimore and Potomac station in Washington, he was shot in the back by assassin Charles Guiteau.

The country anxiously awaited news of Garfield's condition, but after enduring horrendous medical treatments from his doctors, he died from infection eighty days later. Condolences poured in from around the world; even Queen Victoria of England sent a wreath that was displayed on Garfield's casket. According to James A. Garfield National Historic Site manager Dr. Todd Arrington, Lucretia was so touched that she had the wreath preserved in a special wax treatment, and it remains on display at the house today. Garfield was buried in Cleveland's Lake View Cemetery

When the family returned to Mentor, Lawnfield gradually changed. A third floor and back wing were added, which became the James A. Garfield Memorial Library, a forerunner of today's presidential libraries. Years later, family heirs reduced Lawnfield's size to less than eight acres and donated it to the Western Reserve Historical Society in 1936. Congress established the James A. Garfield National Historic Site in 1980 to memorialize Garfield's life.

The Garfield children grew up to be successful in their own right. Harry became president of Williams College and served as Woodrow Wilson's fuel administrator during World War I. James R. became secretary of the interior under President Theodore Roosevelt. Abram worked as a premier architect in northeast Ohio. Irvin became a successful corporate lawyer in Boston. Mary was involved in civic affairs.

President James A. Garfield exhibit panels in Washington, D.C. *Courtesy of National Park Service.*

For years, Garfield was the only president of the four killed in office to not have a marker at the site of his assassination. (The station was demolished in 1907.)

James A. Garfield National Historic Site staff worked with several authors and historians to make historic markers a reality. On November 19, 2018, two exhibit panels about Garfield's life, legacy and assassination were unveiled on the National Mall in Washington, D.C., behind the National Gallery of Art, where the train station used to stand. (The shooting itself took place about five hundred feet away on what is now the very busy Constitution Avenue.)

Hollycroft

Two of Garfield's sons built their homes on either side of Lawnfield. Harry built on what is now Lutheran church property. James R. built a house known as Hollycroft on the other side, although it burned down in the 1960s, and a subdivision now stands along a street bearing the home's name.

Joan Kapsch, park guide at the James A. Garfield National Historic Site, says that when Garfield's descendants recently donated the Hollycroft guest book, staff members discovered an interesting piece of history—the last entries in the book were from English refugees who stayed in the house during World War II.

A *Cleveland Press* article printed on August 2, 1940, explains that James R. Garfield, as secretary of interior in President Theodore Roosevelt's cabinet, had befriended Colonel Bernard James in Washington when he was a military attaché of the British embassy. James R., aware of the escalating war in England, cabled a message to his friend welcoming his grandchildren to seek shelter in his home.

The article reads: "The women, Mrs. Ughtred James and Mrs. Douglas Newbery of Highwycombe, England, both say that, when they left, the interior of their country was still unruffled by the war. It was only because they feared for the safety of their children and for the horrors which the youngsters might have to witness, that they were willing to leave their homeland."

This group included five girls and three boys (from six months to eight years old) accompanied by two mothers (James and Newbery) and two nurses (Katherine Turner and Leonara Zbinden). Two-year-old John Lonsdale was with the group because his mother died when he was born, and his father was a military prisoner in a German camp.

World War II refugees from England sitting on the steps of one of the Garfield homes.
Courtesy of Special Collections, Cleveland State University Library.

They only had five days to prepare for their long and treacherous journey to America and gained passage by chance because James R. discovered that the S.S. *Samaria*, with passenger accommodation for more than two thousand, was to be put into service again.

The group waited hours for official paperwork to be completed and visas assigned and anxiously made a dangerous voyage overseas in a convoy of ships. On the morning of July 2, 1940, off the coast of Ireland, the *Samaria* spotted a passing submarine. It went five miles past the ship and attacked the S.S. *Arandora Star*, which resulted in a great loss of life, with 1,678 passengers on a ship built to carry 500.

James R.'s youngest of four sons, Rudolph Hills, and his wife, Eleanor (who later became mayor of Mentor), lived adjacent to Hollycroft. She prepared the house, which had been closed for four years, for the refugees and helped introduce them to Mentor when they arrived in July 1940.

According to the article, "The youngest are happily settled in their new home. The two older boys are at present visiting in Hanover, N.H. with Mr. Garfield. The other children are enjoying themselves immensely in the enclosed gardens of Mentor. They've already made friends with their nearby neighbors, the King and Baldwin children, and go swimming with them. The four older ones will attend the village school in Mentor with the Garfield children in the fall."

The refugees stayed at the house from 1940 to 1944, when they went back to England on an aircraft carrier captained by a father of one of the refugees.

Staff at the James A. Garfield National Historic Site have recently been in contact with some of the surviving refugees, now in their eighties, living in both England and the United States. Although they were very young when they stayed at Hollycroft, some memories stick out, like visiting with James R., going to the Center Street School, tobogganing in the winter and tapping for maple syrup.

VIOLET CREST

Across the street from Eastlake City Hall, on Lakeshore Boulevard, sits a grand home with pale gray siding and dozens of white-rimmed windows. It fits naturally in its current location but was originally located across the street. (At the time, it was in Willoughby Township, which became Eastlake in the 1940s. The name was picked from 157 resident submissions in a contest to name the city and was narrowed down to three names, including Lakehurst and Lakeland.)

Violet Crest (also known as the Albracht mansion) was built at a cost of $22,043 in 1923 by Conrad "Con" Albracht and his wife, Jessica "Jessie" Balkwill Albracht. They used the five-bedroom house as their summer home

Believed to be Conrad Albracht standing in front of the Albracht cabin. *Courtesy of Eastlake Historical Society.*

and entertained friends and family there for many years. It was named Violet Crest because it was situated on a crest covered in violets. Their property extended from Erie Road along Lakeshore Boulevard to Willowick Drive.

According to a letter written by his nephew Ted in 1979, Conrad worked as a salesman for Cleveland Electric Company when he married his wife. Jessie was the daughter of Washington Ward Balkwill (co-owner of Cleveland Steel Casting Co., one of the top steel castings producers in the United States) and Catherine Breymaier Balkwill. Conrad, who was the son of a German immigrant, later became a successful businessman and owner of K.W. Ignition in Cleveland.

According to Ted, Conrad made $1 million when he sold Henry Ford an order of coils. (His company was well known by Model T owners for manufacturing ignition buzz coils.) He then bought his wife a ten-carat ruby, as he had promised he would when he made his first million.

In 1923, the Albrachts brought a Seminole tribe from Florida to build a cabin, replicating the family's hunting cabin in Canada. It was used as a retreat and for parties and remains tucked behind city hall today, surrounded by overgrowth and, according to the Eastlake Historical Society, in need of restoration.

The City of Eastlake bought the house for $50,000 in 1956, and it housed Eastlake City Hall for thirty-eight years. The police department was also based in the mansion until it moved to a new station next door in 1977. Officers had been using the Violet Crest dinnerware and broke all of the teacups except for one, which is now preserved at the Eastlake Historical Society in city hall. In 1994, city officials moved into a new twenty-six-thousand-square-foot, $2.3 million building.

Also, in 1977, the mansion was moved two thousand feet across Lakeshore Boulevard. It took nine hours to move the three-hundred-ton house, and two ceilings in the main entrance fell out during the move. The main support beam of the house was damaged, but repairs were made, resulting in an enhanced bay window.

At one point, the mansion was at risk of demolition, which would have cost the city $25,000, so officials decided to sell it instead. It was bought at auction, restored to its original grandeur and remains privately owned.

Although furnishings were auctioned off when the city originally bought it, a huge grandfather clock was saved and stands in the entryway of city hall.

KLEIFELD'S RESTAURANT

Kleifeld's Restaurant in downtown Willoughby might not be large, but it's packed full of personality. It's like entering a time capsule, complete with an eight-track jukebox spilling out music from a bygone day. Customers have been enjoying the hot coffee, homemade food and welcoming atmosphere for decades, and many are now in their eighties.

It's the kind of place where you come as a stranger and leave as family, according to owner Kristin Brewster Goodell. And that's what keeps customers coming back again and again.

Kleifeld's Restaurant, open for breakfast and lunch, was established in 1928 as a family-owned and operated business, making it one of the oldest diners in the entire state. However, Kleifeld's started out in a different location in Willoughby. In 1927, P.J. Kleifeld bought one of Willoughby's finest restaurants, called McCarthy's. It quickly became known as Kleifeld's, and when P.J.'s son John Kleifeld took over during the Great Depression, to cut down on overhead costs, he moved the business to its present location on Erie and Third Streets in downtown Willoughby.

Kleifeld's Restaurant with iconic mural on side of building. *Photo by author.*

Kristin, the restaurant's sixth owner, says Ruth Kleifeld was the last original family member to own it, and she sold it in 1968. Kristin says John Kleifeld's niece Karen still sometimes visits the diner to enjoy a hot meal and give her a hug.

Kristin believes part of what makes Kleifeld's special is the storytelling among customers. "You cannot re-create history," says Kristin. "You don't just get breakfast. It comes with an experience and leaves you a little wiser."

Kleifeld's history runs deep to its very old foundation (the Knieling building built in 1888) and the basement that connects it to the neighbors on either side (like many of the businesses in downtown Willoughby). Kristin says it's possible that the basement even connected to buildings across the road through a tunnel at some point (as I have heard from several sources) but doesn't see any evidence of it today. The brick walls of these old buildings have seen a thing or two over the years. Stories of gambling, speakeasies and escape routes abound in this historic part of Willoughby. Kristin also owns Merkel's Flowers, established in the 1940s, which was a mainstay in downtown Willoughby. The basement of the building used to be a bar that was accessed through a discreet alley that led downstairs.

Merkel's moved to a larger space in Mentor shortly before publication of this book.

Much of Kleifeld's Restaurant has been remodeled due to two fires— one in 1953, which resulted in a new stainless steel back bar, which remains in the restaurant today, and a second in 2016, which left the space with a new kitchen.

One of the most iconic parts of the diner is on the outside of the restaurant. The large painted mural on the side of the brick building has been welcoming patrons to downtown Willoughby for decades. It includes a cup of coffee and the saying, "Kleifeld's Restaurant good coffee always." Kristin says it appears in all of the historic photos she has of Kleifeld's and, as far as she knows, has only been touched up once. It's also included in many of the photos that customers take when they come to Kleifeld's for some of life's special events, including marriage proposals, a baby's first outing, wedding photos and senior pictures.

After experiencing a trip to Kleifeld's, with its many characters and hometown feel, you might leave thinking it reminds you of another famous eatery, perhaps the bar on the long-running show *Cheers*.

Television comedy writer Tom Anderson (brother of long-time Willoughby mayor David Anderson) was once a writer for *Cheers* and thought so too. In fact, he knew Kleifeld's was a special place with a story waiting to be told, so he wrote a pilot called "Good Coffee" about the many regulars who visit the diner each day. Although he sold the pilot in Hollywood, it has yet to be produced. Perhaps one day we'll see a version of Kleifeld's turned into a hit TV show.

4

WAR HEROES

CASEMENT-JENNINGS

General John "Jack" S. Casement and his wife, Frances Jennings Casement, were forces to reckon with. They played integral roles in the Civil War, railroad development and in abolitionist and women's suffrage movements.

General Casement was born in Geneva, New York, in 1829. After moving to Michigan with his family and working for the Michigan Central Railroad, he moved to Cleveland in his early twenties and worked as a railroad contractor with his brother Daniel. He met his future wife, seventeen-year-old Frances, while laying tracks for the new Lake Shore Railroad just three hundred yards from her home.

Frances was the youngest daughter of Charles Clement "C.C." Jennings, a congressman from Painesville. When Frances was a baby, C.C. bought three hundred acres of land bordering the east bank of the Grand River from the Connecticut Land Company. A few acres of dense forest were cleared and became Jennings Farm, which included a one-and-a-half-story frame house, a barn and fields for crops. (C.C. played a role in the Underground Railroad, keeping fugitive slaves in his barn overnight and then moving them by wagon, piled with hay, to the lakeshore, where they could make their escape to Canada.)

Jack and Frances married in 1857, and four years later, when the Civil War broke out, Jack enlisted in the army and was appointed major of the

7th Ohio Volunteer Infantry. In his first engagement, he saved four hundred men in a Union defeat, and was promoted to colonel of the newly formed 103rd Ohio Volunteer Regiment a year later after his heroic actions at the Battle of Winchester. He led his regiment in several other pivotal battles and was appointed brigadier general in 1865.

Since Casement was often away from home, he sent letters to Frances. In one, dated October 14, 1861, which was reportedly passed down through the family until going up for public sale, he wrote, "Today is our fourth anniversary. How often I have thought of you today and contrasted our situation today with four years ago. Quite a contrast surely. But darling, one thing is certain. I love you more today than I did then although I thought then that such a thing was impossible."

After the war, Jack and his brother were hired to construct the Union Pacific portion of the Transcontinental Railroad and hired former military personnel to help. Jack became the construction leader and oversaw both the laying of the track and the grading.

Although Jack was only five feet four inches tall, he had a reputation for being quite strong—so strong, in fact, that he was able to move a freight car loaded with rails by pushing his shoulder against the frame.

Under his leadership, 1,087 miles of Union Pacific track was laid from Fremont, Nebraska, to Utah. As soon as the golden spike was hammered, joining the rails at Promontory Point in 1869, Jack hurried home.

In 1870, C.C. built a home for his daughter and son-in-law as a belated wedding gift. It was at the rear of the Jennings cottage, according to a written account by Jack and Frances's granddaughter Mary Casement Furlong, who lived in the home with her family for many years. (Years later, half of the original farmhouse was moved up the road, and the other half was used as a tenant house until the 1960s.)

The Casement House, as it's known today, was designed by Charles W. Heard, son-in-law and student of master builder of the Western Reserve Jonathan Goldsmith. Timber from the property was used to construct the $75,000 Victorian-style building. It took three years to complete. The basement settled for two years before construction began on the rest of the house.

The Casements moved into the home with their young sons, John and Dan, and C.C. Jennings. It was heated and lighted for over forty years by five gas wells dug on the farm, among the first in northern Ohio. Jack was a trustee of nearby Lake Erie Female Seminary (Lake Erie College) and drilled the first gas well on campus to supply heat and light to College Hall

The Casement House. *Courtesy of R.W. Sidley, Inc. and the Sidley Family.*

so that they could stop using soft coal, which left black particles of soot in the water and soiled the students' clothes.

The Casement House had its own "air conditioning," thanks to wooden ducts built into the walls to carry stale air out and draw in cool air from outside.

Both Frances's father and husband were well-known abolitionists, and while building the railroad, Jack was elected to the U.S. Congress as a nonvoting representative from the Wyoming Territory. During this time, Frances also became a supporter for women's suffrage and met Elizabeth Cady Stanton and Susan B. Anthony when they lobbied with her husband for women's rights and Wyoming statehood.

In 1883, Frances founded the Painesville Equal Rights Association and was president of the Ohio Woman Suffrage Association for three years, working to ease the differences between the major national suffragist societies, the National Woman Suffrage Association and the American Woman Suffrage Association. They eventually merged in 1890, forming the National American Woman Suffrage Association, which incorporated many of her ideas.

According to their granddaughter Mary Casement Furlong, in letters courtesy of the Sidley family, the Casement House was often filled with friends, comrades from railroad ventures, fellow soldiers from the Civil War and women suffrage leaders like Susan B. Anthony and Elizabeth Cady Stanton (who often slept in the north bedrooms furnished with rosewood and curly maple).

Mary said that perhaps their largest gathering was on July 3 and 4, 1874, when General Jack invited veterans of his old regiment to a reunion. Comrades and their wives danced on the front lawn, and General James A. Garfield addressed the crowd at Painesville Park. There weren't enough beds, so visitors slept on the floor, on the porches, in the barns and in tents on the lawn.

Until 1885, General Jack was said to have laid more track than any other railroad contractor in the world. In addition to laying the Union Pacific, he constructed the

General Jack Casement. *Courtesy of Special Collections, Cleveland State University Library.*

rails of the Lake Shore Railroad from Cleveland to Erie, the Big Four from Cleveland to Columbus and the Nickel Plate from Cleveland to Buffalo. He also spent three years building a railroad in the rainforest of Costa Rica.

He died in 1909 at the age of eighty-one, and Frances died in 1928 at eighty-eight, having lived to see women get the right to vote when Congress passed the Nineteenth Amendment in 1920.

After Jack and Frances died, their son Dan, a well-known cattle rancher in the West, received the house through General Casement's will. When Dan died in 1953, prominent businessman and community leader Robert W. Sidley and his wife, Edith, purchased the house and three-hundred-acre farm from his estate. They bought back a lot of the home's original furniture that was auctioned off and modernized the home with electrical lighting and lead pipes.

According to R.W. Sidley's oldest grandchild, Robert J. Buescher, the Sidley family moved to the Casement farm from Madison. They owned, R.W. Sidley Inc., mining sand and gravel on the property for about fifty years, supplying the local construction industry with ready mix concrete. The building currently houses the company's executive offices.

COOK CLELAND

Tucked away behind Dunkin' Donuts on Euclid Avenue in Willoughby is the shell of an old airport hangar. The dome-shaped building on East 355th Street was once part of Cook Cleland Airport, sometimes also known as Euclid Avenue Airport.

It's one of four Willoughby airports that were busy aviation hot spots in the 1930s and '40s, along with Chagrin Harbor Airport (once located on the southeast corner of Lake Shore Boulevard and the Chagrin River), Willoughby Airport (once located between Mentor Avenue and Ridge Road) and Lost Nation Airport (located on Lost Nation Road and still active today).

The airport was named after Cook Cleland, born in Cleveland on Christmas Eve 1916, who dreamed of flying as a young boy. After graduating from Shaw High School in East Cleveland, he attended the University of Missouri, where he met his future wife, Ora Lee. Cook then began his lifelong journey in aviation when he joined the navy in 1940, got married

Cook Cleland's Euclid Avenue Airport, 1940s. *Courtesy of Willoughby Historical Society.*

Cook Cleland in the cockpit of a Corsair in 1946. *Courtesy of Special Collections, Cleveland State University Library.*

and continued to train in Pensacola, Florida. He became an accomplished "ace" after qualifying as a dive bomber pilot in World War II. He received the Navy Cross during World War II after sinking a Japanese aircraft carrier during a dive bomb and leading his section on a long and hazardous night journey back to base. He also participated in every major Pacific engagement, except Midway, until the summer of 1944.

After the war, he evaluated enemy aircraft as a navy test pilot in Lexington Park, Maryland, and then returned to the Cleveland area. Cook worked at Thompson Products, which produced aircraft parts, and the company later sponsored the Thompson Trophy at the air races.

Cook then acquired a small airport in Willoughby, established between 1929 and 1932, and renamed it Cook Cleland's Euclid Avenue Airport. Dick Becker, who flew PBY Catalina and Martin PBM Mariner patrol bomber flying boats (the world's largest twin-engine flying boat) for the navy in the South Pacific, joined him in the venture.

Originally known as Euclid Avenue Airport, it was depicted as a commercial/municipal airport in the December 1932 Cleveland Sectional

Chart and was said to consist of two runways spanning a one-hundred-acre rectangular sod field. By 1934, the airport was described as having three runways and a hangar on the southwest side of the field, with "Euclid Avenue Airport" painted on the roof. By 1937, that changed again, and the roof was said to read "Euclid Avenue Air Service."

During this time, Cleland offered air charters, banner towing and flying lessons. He wanted to expand his air charter service, so he bought several surplus PBYs. To be certified for commercial use, the FAA required several modifications, including aluminum firewalls to be replaced with stainless steel, fabric on two-thirds of the wing had to be replaced with metal and the controls needed to be moved from the pylon to the cockpit. When modifications were complete, Cook sold one but used the others for his new service, called Cook Cleland's Catalina Airways, to carry passengers to Kodiak, Alaska, for hunting and fishing trips. His flying boat was said to be painted cream on top with a deep green on the bottom, separated by a metallic bronze feature stripe.

In 1946, Cook entered the Cleveland National Air Races, with help from the Thompson Products employees. He bought one of the first surplus Corsairs—a FG-1D built by Goodyear in Akron. He entered ex-navy Corsairs in four postwar races and began racing in the Cleveland National Air Races. After buying three F2G Corsairs, his flying dreams came true when he won the coveted Thompson Trophy in 1947, at thirty years old, and again in 1949 (the year the Cleveland Sectional Chart labeled the field as "Cook Cleland," though the name wouldn't last much longer).

The 1949 National Air Races drew 170,000 spectators over the course of Labor Day weekend. The races began with excitement but ended in tragedy on Monday, September 5, the final day. They were held at the Cleveland Municipal Airport for the twelfth time since the air races began in 1929, and this also became their last time on the site.

One of the racers in the Thompson Trophy Race, the day's major event, was William Paul "Bill" Odom. He was flying a radically modified North American Aviation P-51 C Mustang, named *Beguine*, owned by the famous aviatrix Jacqueline "Jackie" Cochran. (It had been named by a previous owner after Cole Porter's "Begin the Beguine.")

The race included fifteen laps around a seven-turn, fifteen-mile course and was marked by a tall pylon at the airport. Odom had never flown in this kind of race but was known for a number of long-distance record flights. He quickly took the lead when the race began, but on the second lap, as he approached Pylon 4, *Beguine* rolled upside and crashed into a home in

Cook Cleland after winning the Thompson Trophy. *Courtesy of Special Collections, Cleveland State University Library.*

Berea, setting the house on fire. Jeanne Laird was inside and died instantly, while her thirteen-month-old son, Craig, passed away later at the Berea Community Hospital. Her husband and five-year-old son survived because they had been standing outside watching the planes.

Despite the crash, the races continued, with Cook Cleland winning the race in his clip-winged Corsair, but the tragedy marked the end of closed-course racing in this residential area. After twenty years, the National Air Races came to an end. (Cleveland wouldn't host another air show until 1964, when the modern style of show began at Burke Lakefront Airport.)

After the air race, business began to slow at Cook Cleland Airport, Cook gave up his lease and it closed in the early 1950s. The land along the east boundary of the property on Beidler Road was sold to small shops and businesses. (Buildings stand on the old airport fields today, and the old hangar is owned by a private business.)

Cook then returned to active duty in the Korean War as a commanding officer of carrier-based Fighting Squadron 653. He continued to fly the Chance-Vought F4U Corsair in sixty-seven combat missions over North Korea and managed to make it through both World War II and the Korean War unscathed.

He continued working as a test pilot in the navy and was stationed in Alaska for a while, where he rose to the rank of captain. In 1967, Cook retired from the navy and moved to Pensacola, Florida, where he gave flight lessons and flew until he was eighty.

Besides aviation, his other love was history, and he and his wife started an antique business when he was still in the navy. They opened a shop in Pensacola called Cleland Antiques and happily ran it for many years. They also raised three children and enjoyed visiting with their grandchildren and great-grandchildren.

In 2000, Cook was inducted into the Motor Sports Hall of Fame in Detroit, Michigan. He died in Pensacola on July 13, 2007, at the age of ninety.

Margaret Hurlburt

Aviatrix Margaret "Marge" Hurlburt of Painesville was known as the Queen of the Air. She was a pioneer in women's aviation, with deep roots in Lake County.

Marge was born in Painesville on December 30, 1914, graduated from Harvey High School in 1932 and went on to earn a degree in education from Bowling Green State University. She taught English for several years, all the while dreaming of soaring through the skies, so she began taking lessons at the Euclid Avenue Airport in Willoughby and eventually earned her private pilot license.

She decided to join the World War II effort in 1942 and was recruited by Jacqueline "Jackie" Cochran, famed aviatrix and founder of the Women Airforce Service Pilots (WASPs). When Hurlburt finished basic training, Cochran presented her with her WASP wings at Avenger Field in Sweetwater, Texas.

Cochran started the WASPs in the early days of the war, working with General Hap Arnold, who was chief of army air forces, to fill an urgent wartime need—transporting newly built military planes that were quickly rolling off assembly lines to the military bases, since most male pilots were already at war.

To become a WASP, a woman needed to be at least eighteen years old and have a private pilot's license and at least two hundred hours of flying time. For several years, Hurlburt proudly ferried aircraft and bravely towed targets for B-24 gunners.

When the WASP program was deactivated in 1944, its members didn't receive the benefits that the returning veterans got. Although they collectively had more than sixty million air miles, in many ways, history ignored them. In 1977, Congress finally declared them veterans, and two years later, air force officials accepted the same status.

When her job with the WASP program was over, Hurlburt convinced several former colleagues to join her in Ohio to obtain their flight instructor ratings.

Rose Moore, member of the International Women's Air and Space Museum (IWASM), located at Burke Lakefront Airport in Cleveland, wrote about Hurlburt's return to Willoughby in a blog post. When the now-deceased Herb Tanner of Tanner Flying Service in Willoughby was eighty-nine years old, he told Rose about the day Hurlburt and her friends arrived at Chagrin Harbor Airport, which he was managing.

"I saw a cloud of dust moving down the road, and from it emerged a convertible full of pretty young women," he recalled. "I had posted a sign for instructors, and these five women were there to apply. I jumped at the chance and hired them all. They were bright, and Marge was the brightest. She could fly anything from B-17s to the little single-seaters at our field. I signed her on to teach ground school and meteorology too!"

In 1946, Hurlburt, who was ahead of her time in many ways, was the only woman still on staff, and pilots Gil Cargill and Dick Cook began teaching her aerobatics in an AT-6. When she wanted to sign up to compete in the women's Halle Trophy Race at the Cleveland Air Races, Tanner paid the seventy-five-dollar fee for her to enter; Thematic Co., of Willoughby, paid for the plane's gas; and Cargill and Cook waxed and polished the AT-6 and continued to teach Hurlburt about the nuances of pylon racing.

Margaret Hurlburt with Lucky Gallon, the FG-1 Corsair she flew to break the women's speed record in 1947. *Courtesy of the International Women's Air & Space Museum.*

Hurlburt won the race and, looking the part of a glamorous aviatrix in a designer flight suit from New York, accepted her trophy and $2,500 cash from Samuel Halle, race sponsor and owner of one of Cleveland's leading department stores of the time. She continued to soar in the world of women's aviation when she was named to the board of directors of the Professional Race Pilots Association as a representative for female pilots.

In Tampa, Florida, in 1947, Hurlburt experienced one of her greatest moments as a pilot when she set an international women's flight speed record, of 337.635 miles per hour, beating Jackie Cochran, who had held the title for a decade at 292.27 miles per hour. She was racing in an FG-1 Corsair that she borrowed from her friend and fellow-air racer Cook Cleland of Willoughby. In recognition of the Painesville businesspeople who sponsored her during the race, she had the plane painted with "City of Painesville" across its side, and it was later displayed in the town square. A few weeks later, a banquet was held at the historic Rider's Inn to celebrate her achievement, and April 24–26 were proclaimed Marge Hurlburt Days.

Marge Hurlburt in Lucky Gallon with "City of Painesville, Ohio" written along the side. *Courtesy of International Women's Air & Space Museum.*

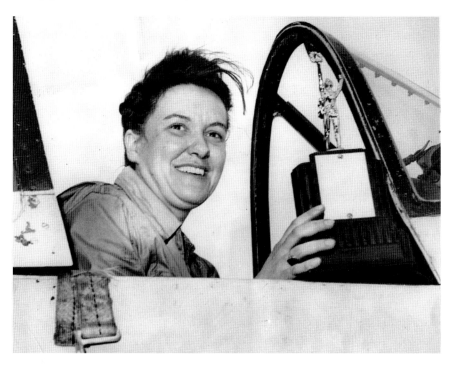

Marge Hurlburt with the trophy for setting the international women's speed record in 1947. *Courtesy of International Women's Air & Space Museum.*

Marge was dubbed "America's Queen of the Air" by the media, and Chance Voight, builder of the Corsair, described her racing performance as "slightly on the miraculous side."

Hurlburt's next goal was to compete for the $25,000 prize at the Goodyear Trophy Race in Cleveland, but to sign up, she needed to come up with money, so she decided to join an aerial circus called the Flying Tigers. Tragically, Hurlburt never got to participate in the Goodyear race. On July 4, 1947, in Decorah, Iowa, while in the middle of an air stunt in a borrowed AT-6, her plane dived and crashed into a cornfield, and she was killed instantly at just thirty-two years old. Her death made national news and was listed in the July 14 Milestones section of *Time* magazine.

She is buried at Painesville's Evergreen Cemetery and is remembered with a rose-colored tombstone etched with an airplane and the WASP initials. Marge was posthumously awarded the Congressional Gold Medal on March 10, 2010, along with many other women who were finally recognized for their contributions as members of the WASP program during World War II.

Nearly seventy-five years later, she is remembered for being a fearless leader in women's aviation. Many of her memorabilia and artifacts are on display at IWASM, including the gold medal, which her family donated. The museum also has other interesting pieces from Hurlburt's life and flying career, including her leather flying helmet, pilot licenses, logbook and the small hand puppet from her childhood that had been her good luck charm on every flight, including her last.

EARL LANE

Earl Roscoe Lane, of Wickliffe, is a war hero who fought for not only our nation during World War II but also his own equality. As the only Tuskegee Airman from Lake County, he helped pave the wave for the integration of the U.S. Armed Forces.

Before World War II, the U.S. Army Air Corps (AAC), a precursor of the U.S. Air Force, did not employ Black men, but that changed in 1940, when President Franklin D. Roosevelt ordered the creation of an all-Black flying unit. It would become known as the Tuskegee Airmen, named for the training grounds at the Tuskegee Army Air Field in Alabama.

The Tuskegee Airmen flew more than fifteen thousand combat sorties in over 1,578 missions during World War II and earned more than 150

Members of the Tuskegee 332nd Fighter Group in a briefing room in Ramitelli, Italy. Earl Lane is believed to be at the bottom far left. *Courtesy of Library of Congress.*

Distinguished Flying Crosses. They also paved the way for desegregation of the military after the war, with President Harry Truman's executive order mandating equality of opportunity and treatment in the U.S. Armed Forces.

First Lieutenant Lane was born on July 22, 1920, in Redbird, Oklahoma, a town formed by Black people after the Civil War, where they could live with economic independence. When Lane was ten years old, at the start of the Great Depression, he moved to Wickliffe with his parents, Levi and Christine, and sister Barbara, and they built their family home on Robindale Avenue. (Levi Lane had served in World War I and was a Civil Rights activist and important humanitarian in the city of Wickliffe for decades.

Years after serving as a Tuskegee Airman, Earl Lane worked as deputy housing coordinator for the Cuyahoga County welfare department. *Courtesy of Special Collections, Cleveland State University Library.*

Civic Park was renamed Levi Lane Park in 2002 in honor of his dedication to the residents of the city.)

In April 1944, Earl graduated with his Tuskegee Airman Class and within a year, he was a major player in one of the most significant events in Tuskegee Airman history.

During the war, fifty-five airmen were credited with destroying 112 German aircraft in the air, and on March 24, 1945, the Tuskegee airmen shot down three German jets.

Lieutenant Lane, who flew with the 332nd Fighter Group (the Redtails), was one of three airmen credited with shooting down three Messerschmitt Me 262 (German fighter jets) the first over Berlin, Germany. They were escorting heavy bombers to their target in Berlin, a massive Daimler-Benz tank factory, when they were confronted by the Me 262s launched by the Jagdgeschwader 7 (Fighter Group 7) "Nowotny" from Brandenburg Briest.

Although the American P-51s were typically slower than the German planes, they could outmaneuver them and had much better fuel retention. First Lieutenant Lane, First Lieutenant Roscoe Brown and Second Lieutenant Charles Brantley all shot down German jets over Berlin that day.

According to Defense Media Network, First Lieutenant Earl R. Lane had extraordinary eyesight and scored his victory from a two-thousand-yard distance in a deflection shot while in a tight, left-hand turn, using the relatively new K-14 lead-computing gunsight to lead far ahead of the jet. His adversary, "a jet with a steel blue-gray camouflage," Lane wrote later, was piloted by seven-kill ace Second Lieutenant Alfred Ambs.

Lane said of the moment, "He did not quite fill my gunsight. I fired three short bursts and saw the plane emitting smoke. A piece of the plane, either the canopy or one of the jet orifices, flew off. I then pulled up and circled over the spot where he went down. I saw a crash and a puff of black smoke. Two seconds later, I saw another piece hit close to the first piece. I was at 17,000 feet when I broke off the encounter." (Lieutenant Ambs survived the shots. After bailing out at 17,000 feet, he became entangled in the branches of a tree and lived a long life but never fought again.)

Lieutenants Lane, Brown and Brantley's 332nd Fighter Group later received a Distinguished Unit Citation for their heroic efforts participating in the longest bomber escort mission in World War II. In total, Lane was awarded eight medals during his time as a Tuskegee Airman, including the Distinguished Flying Cross.

Lane returned to Wickliffe after the war and enrolled at Cleveland State University, where he went on to graduate with a degree from the John Marshall School of Law. He worked for Cuyahoga County in a variety of jobs over the years, including as a social worker, a probation officer and for the welfare department, until he retired in 1979.

He continued to fly planes until the late '70s, when he was forced to stop due to health conditions, but his love of flying never diminished. Lieutenant Lane passed away years later, on June 27, 1990, but the role he played in Tuskegee Airman history is just as important today.

5

NOTABLE RESIDENTS

JONATHAN GOLDSMITH

If you've ever meandered through Lake County admiring buildings that are remnants of the pioneer age, you've likely laid eyes on a Jonathan Goldsmith. He, arguably, more than any other architect/builder played the biggest role in developing our region in its earliest days.

Jonathan Goldsmith, a veteran of the War of 1812 and inventor and patent holder of the multiple plow, is recognized for bringing the early Greek revival movement to the Western Reserve. In Lake County alone he built about forty cottages and mansions, four taverns, a lighthouse, a business block, a bank, a school and, with Grand Newell, a railway.

Goldsmith was born several states away, in Connecticut, in 1783. His father, Captain Jonathan Gillett Goldsmith, died of smallpox when Jonathan was only eleven years old, after sailing home from a trip to the West Indies. Since Jonathan's mother, Anna Beers Goldsmith, was left to support him and his two sisters, she moved her family to New Haven and got Jonathan an apprenticeship with a shoemaker. He was supposed to continue until he was twenty-one but never liked the work, so he bought off his remaining four years when he was seventeen and apprenticed himself to a carpenter-joiner instead.

He quickly excelled at the trade and moved to Massachusetts and started his own business. He built a home, where he lived with his wife, Abigail, and her mother, Jemima Skinner Jones, while her father, Benaiah Jones, was in Ohio overseeing construction of a log house for their family.

Abigail's uncle Captain Abraham Skinner was a land agent for the Connecticut Land Company. He helped General Henry Champion (a director of the Connecticut Land Company and brother-in-law of Moses Cleaveland) secure land in this new frontier. The Champion holdings spanned a ridge overlooking the Grand River not far from Lake Erie. Champion laid out a village green and several streets, which quickly became known as Champion. (When General Paine later moved to the territory, it was renamed Painesville after him.)

Champion urged the Goldsmiths to move to this area (along with sixty of Abigail's relatives). It took the Goldsmiths, with their daughters, two-year-old Caroline and six-month-old Eliza, the entire month of June 1811 to make the five-hundred-mile journey by horse and wagon. After arriving in Ohio, they had a very close call while crossing over the Ashtabula River gorge on an open plank bridge. Their oxen suddenly began dragging their covered wagon within a tire's width of the edge of the bridge, but they were luckily able to safely get back on land.

At first, Jonathan's main source of income in Champion was mending shoes, but as soon as he built a log cabin for his family, on Mentor Avenue in Painesville, his job as a builder took off because people could see the fine example of his work from the road.

By 1818, his family of eight ran out of space in their original log cabin. Jonathan began building the Old Homestead, a larger frame house. Jonathan, described as a man of medium height with blue eyes and a prominent ridge on his nose, was in demand to build homes, stores and taverns. Men and women enjoyed the dance floors he installed, which were some of the first "sprung floors" (one floor laid crosswise over another to give the dancers extra bounce) in the Western Reserve.

Although Goldsmith was busy with his work, he was devoted to his wife and family. As the story goes, in 1829, when Goldsmith told his wife he wanted to move to Jonesville, Michigan, Abigail simply replied, "I think I won't." So, they didn't.

By 1835, the Goldsmiths had filled their second home with their now ten children and an apprentice who often lived with them.

Goldsmith also worked on the Painesville & Fairport Railroad. However, it never went past Painesville and eventually went bankrupt. It stopped running altogether when the trestle at the Grand River was carried away in the spring flood of 1841. Around the same time, Jonathan ended up losing

$1,200 in a bad business deal with a man known only as "Mr. B," who turned out to be a swindler. The loss was so significant that he had to sell the Old Homestead and eighty-six acres of land.

In 1843, Goldsmith built his family a smaller home in Painesville, which was his last building. He died in 1847 at the age of 64 and was buried at the Painesville Township cemetery, close to his farm. Abigail outlived him by four decades and celebrated her 100th birthday at Ingleside, as this last house came to be called. Their daughter Lucia ended up living in the home until she was 87 years old, when she moved in with her niece. The home stood on the current site of the Lake County Fairground until it burned down in 1929.

Jonathan Goldsmith's legacy is still evident in the buildings, with his trademark fluted molding and corner blocks that have been restored and also those falling into ruin, waiting for their chance to shine once again.

Harry Coulby

Wickliffe City Hall on Ridge Road was once the grand estate of millionaire businessman Harry C. Coulby. As a young boy in England, he dreamed of sailing the Great Lakes, used all of his savings to sail to America and eventually landed in Wickliffe, becoming the "Czar of the Great Lakes."

Coulby's journey began in Claypole, England, where he was born in 1865. He grew up in a large family on a farm and learned the value of hard work at a young age, even dropping out of school at eleven to become a farm laborer. Perhaps it was that early work ethic that helped him succeed when he immigrated to America at just seventeen years old.

While working as a railroad telegrapher in Cuba, Coulby became very sick with malaria. He couldn't get medical help, so he used his savings to board a steamship to New York City, where nuns at a Catholic hospital nursed him back to health. Years later, he returned their kindness with many donations to Catholic causes.

Next, Coulby was hoping to make his dream come true by heading to Ohio.

In a 1923 interview in the *American Magazine*, Coulby said, "As a boy in England, I had read about the Great Lakes; inland seas that make our English lakes seem like mere ponds. You can understand how this appealed to the imagination of a boy who had seen as little of the world as I had. The name itself—the 'Great Lakes'—fascinated me. So when I came to

Coulby Mansion. *Photo by author.*

America it was with a well-formed plan in mind. I wanted to see those lakes! If possible, I was going to sail them."

According to *Cleveland: The Making of a City*, Coulby asked a New York police officer how to get there and was told, "You're on Broadway, boy. Keep walking west for five hundred miles." He walked westward along the New York Central tracks for six weeks, picking up odd jobs along the way to pay for food and boarding.

He reached Cleveland in 1883, at a pivotal time. Pickands Mather & Company, a chief supplier of raw materials to the steel industry, with headquarters in Cleveland, was a source of great opportunity for European immigrants looking for work on the Great Lakes. Coulby was perhaps the most ambitious of them all.

First, he tried to work as a ship hand on the SS *Onoko* but was turned down due to lack of experience. Next, he worked in construction, wearing boots donated by a fellow laborer, and studied shorthand at night. This led to a job as a secretary to the president of the Lake Shore and Michigan Southern Railway. After failing to get a raise from his forty-dollar-a-month paycheck, Coulby responded to a newspaper advertisement placed by John Hay, the former secretary to President Abraham Lincoln and future U.S. secretary of state.

Hay hired Coulby to transcribe his twelve-volume biography of Lincoln and offered him a job in Washington, D.C., when it was completed. Instead, Coulby accepted a job offer from Samuel Mather to work as a clerk at Pickands Mather for fifty dollars a month. As history would dictate, it proved to be a good choice.

Coulby quickly mastered the business from navigation to freight rates. Within a decade, he was coordinating company shipping facilities from Buffalo to Duluth and building up the fleet. He also proudly became an American citizen. By 1904, Coulby was managing more than one hundred ships, including a massive fleet at the newly formed U.S. Steel, along with ships at Pickands Mather. He was dubbed the Czar of the Great Lakes and even had a steamship named after him.

In 1910, Coulby divorced his first wife, Jane Coulby, alleging that her abusive language made it impossible to keep servants in their home. Shortly

SS *Harry Coulby*, 1906. *Courtesy of Library of Congress.*

after, he met May Allen Scott, the widow of a Civil War doctor, and they married in 1911.

They purchased a plateau in Wickliffe Township with sweeping views of Lake Erie. Knowing that his partner, Samuel Mather, had just built his mansion on Euclid Avenue's Millionaires' Row in Cleveland, Coulby asked Cleveland architect Frederic W. Striebinger to build him "the most beautiful home in Ohio." His $1 million mansion was completed in 1915, after two years of construction, and was named Coulallenby, combining his name with that of his wife's.

Coulby was said to keep the trees trimmed in front of his room in the east wing to have a clear view of his ships out on Lake Erie. By the end of 1916, in the middle of World War I, the Great Lakes fleets had allegedly carried sixty-five million tons of iron ore, filling an insatiable demand by the United States.

Coulby became Wickliffe Township's first mayor in 1916, with only one vote against him—his opponent's. He didn't accept a salary and even personally paid for the town's streetlights.

Coulby never forgot his roots and returned to England each Christmas with gifts and a load of coal for residents of Claypole. According to the Wickliffe Historical Society, he paid for renovations for the town's church, donated to the nearby hospital, built his sister a home and financed a new village hall, considered one of the best in Britain.

Coulby's wife died in 1921, and he passed away in 1929, at the age of sixty-four, while visiting his siblings in his English birthplace. He was buried at the churchyard that he had restored. After his death, his generosity lived on in his $4.1 million estate, providing funds for relatives, the Village of Claypole, Coulallenby employees and college scholarships for the children of Pickands Mather employees. The Cleveland Foundation received a $3 million gift, making it one of the largest community trusts in the world. In recent years, his hometown even named a new subdivision Wickliffe Park in honor of Coulby's much-loved Ohio home.

Coulallenby went on to house a girls' boarding school in the 1930s. It was started by the Sisters of Holy Humility of Mary and passed through several other owners before the City of Wickliffe took over in 1954. Today it houses the administrative offices of Wickliffe City Hall, including the mayor's office and Wickliffe Historical Society.

CHARLES OTIS

One of the oldest buildings in Waite Hill is a Victorian-style house in the middle of the village. It was built in the 1870s by one of the foremost farmers in the area, George H. Hoose. According to a newspaper article, Hoose was quite a showman: "George Hoose of Waite Hill, on November 10, 1879, husked 122 bu. of corn inside of ten hours. Took the shocks down, husked them, tied up the shocks and set them up as fast as they were husked. Didn't do it on a wager, just for recreation."

George built the home for his parents, Cornelius and Jane Hoose, and moved to their former farmhouse with his family on the seventy-acre property when it was completed.

The farm, originally owned by pioneer Luther Waite—the youngest son of early settlers William D. and Speedy Waite, was known for its perfectly-tilled fields of clover and grain and well-trimmed apple and peach orchards.

In the early 1900s, businessman Charles A. Otis Jr. bought the property from the Hooses and named it Tannenbaum Farm. The house, still standing today, was used as a boardinghouse for men working on the farm and was conveniently located next to the barns where he raised pigs, cows, turkeys and eventually racehorses. (There's even a half-mile track at the back of the property spanning several privately owned pieces of land.) His purchase made him one of the first large landowners in Waite Hill.

Otis, born in Cleveland in 1868, was one of the most influential business leaders in the region around the turn of the century. His father was president of Otis Steel and was elected mayor of Cleveland in 1873. As a young man, Otis, nicknamed Tot, spent several years working in the cattle business out West with his good friend and son of General Jack Casement, Dan Casement.

Otis later graduated from Yale University and mentioned in his autobiography, *Here I Am*, that he began running into childhood friend Lucia at social events after returning home to Cleveland. They later married, with Casement as best man, honeymooned in Europe for a year and lived downtown after returning to Cleveland. Otis entered the iron and steel brokerage business and organized Otis, Hough, & Company, leading to the establishment of the Cleveland Stock Exchange. In 1899, he purchased the first seat held by an Ohioan on the New York Stock Exchange while organizing the Cleveland Stock Exchange.

After Otis and Lucia's first child, William, was born, the doctor suggested they keep him away from the polluted air of Cleveland, so they moved to Waite Hill in 1901 and started farming.

"People were then beginning to look toward the country with longing eyes, aspiring to be city farmers—town in winter and the country in summer," Otis explained. Otis purchased about a mile on the north side of Waite Hill and twenty acres on the south. Several years later, their daughter, Lucia, was born.

On a snowy February day, Otis's good friend John "Jack" Sherwin, a leading businessman and philanthropist, visited him. "I showed him the layout and he became infatuated with a country place," Otis recalled. "He eventually bought nearly all of the south side of Waite Hill, and called it his South Farm. Mine was called Tannenbaum Farm at that time because there were pine trees all around and Willie always sang 'Tannenbaum, Dear Tannenbaum,' as his Fraulein had taught him all the German songs. We changed the name to 'Pine Tree Farm' during the First World War."

Otis was involved in the Cleveland steel industry, was president of the Cuyahoga Telephone Company, helped develop the phone business we know today (connecting the independents with Ohio Bell Telephone Company, which grew into AT&T) and purchased an evening paper, the *Cleveland World*. He consolidated the evening editions of two other papers to create the *Cleveland News*, becoming the city's only evening paper.

"I remember how I frequently went to a dinner party, was blamed for the telephone service, for the actions of the stock market, and criticized for the position the newspaper took on most any subject," he said.

Pine Tree Farm. *Courtesy of* Here I Am *by Charles A. Otis.*

When he sold the *News* to his friend Dan Hanna Sr., their binding contract was simply a blank telegraph sheet. On it, Hanna wrote, "Tot agrees to sell me the *News* for a million dollars less certain things." According to Otis, the contract was framed and hung in the newspaper's office.

Otis was a busy man but always enjoyed retreating to the peaceful serenity of Pine Tree Farm. He helped organize a number of social clubs, including the Tavern Club, the Kirtland Country Club and Chagrin Valley Hunt Club (organized in a barn on his Waite Hill property, which still stands and is privately owned).

On one of Otis's more memorable visits to Kirtland Country Club, he danced with the visiting Amelia Earhart. In *Here I Am*, Otis explains, "And she said, 'Mr. Otis, I wonder if we are related. My mother was Judge Otis' daughter who moved to Missouri where she married my father.'"

Otis asked her to join him and his wife for breakfast at their home the following morning so that he could show her his research of the Otis family tree. When he opened his large book, he pointed to a picture of Earhart's mother, who was a second cousin of his father.

During one visit to Cleveland, Earhart requested that Otis bring her an Irish terrier to fly beside her as a mascot, which he did. He said that before Earhart started on her last trip, she had large tires put on her plane in Akron and visited Pine Tree Farm. According to Otis, she showed them the map of her planned flight over the Pacific with a red circle around an island that held her supplies and refueling equipment for the last stretch.

"I recall remarking to Amelia, 'If you should miss that island, you will certainly be in a dickens of a fix.' But she insisted she would hit it and that everything would be okay. But I had a feeling that in that vast expanse of water and desolate islands something disastrous would happen, and I really did all I could to dissuade her from the flight, as did her husband. However, she was determined to make the jump, explaining what it would mean in the advancement of aviation, which of course was her entire life," Otis stated.

The Otises lived on the farm for decades. Charles retired in 1931 but stayed involved in civic and philanthropic causes. He died more than two decades later, in 1953.

Over the years, his property had several prominent owners, including William H. Staples, who, after extensively remodeling the home Otis used as a boardinghouse, ran into financial trouble and left in the dead of night, never to return. In the 1950s, several subsidiaries of Textron Inc., where William Staples had worked, bought the property and divided it into two parcels.

Charles A. Otis giving Amelia Earhart an Irish Terrier. *Courtesy of* Here I Am *by Charles A. Otis.*

One parcel, including the Victorian-style house, was long and narrow, allowing access to a spring in the back. Waite Hill resident Emile Legros, officer of Textron and founder of Cedar Point amusement park in Sandusky, eventually bought the other parcel.

Janet Dodge Garfield, widow of President James A. Garfield's grandson John Newell, lived in the home from 1953 until her death in 1959. She was said to signal to her friend and neighbor Charles McCahill with the shade in her first-floor bedroom. If the shade was up, he was invited for cocktails, but if it was down, then he was not.

The historic home has been privately owned and meticulously cared for since then, preserving its historic integrity at the center of the Waite Hill community.

AMY KAUKONEN

From the late 1800s to the early 1900s, Fairport was a rough-and-tumble place. It was a busy lake port entry filled with dock workers who liked their alcohol, which often led to seedy behavior.

There were twenty-one saloons and two breweries in Fairport in 1901, but all had closed by 1906. Of the businesses that remained open, including hotels, pool halls and restaurants (often operating as saloons), 90 percent were still openly selling bootleg whiskey during the years of Prohibition, from 1920 to 1933. Speakeasies were popular establishments named after the bartenders asking patrons to "speak easy" or quietly while ordering their illegal drinks. Fairport had achieved a reputation as a bootlegger's paradise. It was often referred to as a "damp spot on the lake," thanks to the easy access Lake Erie provided to Canada, which kept alcohol flowing freely across the lake.

Residents were getting tired of the rowdy behavior and feared that their neighborhoods would continue to decline if something wasn't done to stop it. It reached a peak in 1921, when two men (police officers, according to some articles of the time) died by murder/suicide in a bar fight involving bootleg liquor.

Earlier that day, a young local doctor, Dr. Amy Kaukonen, had even warned one of the men that they would die of liver failure if they didn't stop drinking. Kaukonen had witnessed many medical maladies that were a result of the overconsumption of alcohol. She was a staunch opponent of bootlegging and its ill effects.

When she heard about the deaths of the two men, and on the urging of other women in the village, she decided she would be the one to make a positive change and would run for mayor of Fairport in 1921.

Although her parents were born in Finland, they immigrated to the United States in 1889, and Amy was born in Lorain, Ohio, in 1891. She was only twenty-nine years old in 1920, when she started her own medical practice in Fairport. She had graduated with honors from the Women's Medical College in Philadelphia, Pennsylvania, and settled in Fairport, where about half of the village residents were Finnish.

With support from much of the community, she ran as a candidate of the Reform party, which was unofficially against alcohol, dance halls and a corrupt government. According to the December 1922 edition of *Current Opinion*, Kaukonen summarized her platform, saying, "I'm out to clean up Fairport. I'm only one little woman, but this town is going to have its face, neck and ears washed before I get through with it."

Dr. Amy Kaukonen. *Courtesy of Finnish Heritage Museum.*

Election night was described in the same *Current Opinion*:

> *Crowds swirled and eddied around the Kaukonen home. Horns tooted, sirens screamed outside. Inside, a slip of a golden-haired girl sat reading, one hand snuggled in the shaggy collar of the faithful canine of the family. Her mother, Mrs. Caroline Kaukonen, waited, too, but she did not read. It*

102

was nearly morning when the phone rang. The girl marked her book and answered it. "Good evening, Your Honor," said a voice. "You have been elected mayor of the village of Fairport by a majority too great to count." Hardly had the girl mayor-elect left the phone before bedlam swept the town and congratulations poured in.

In 1921, she won by seventy-five votes (465 to 390) against William Stange, just one year after the passage of the Nineteenth Amendment, which gave women the right to vote. She was the first woman to be elected mayor in Ohio and among the first in the country.

Once in office, she was frustrated that the reelected marshal, J.H. Werbeach, continued to turn a blind eye to bootlegger activities, so Kaukonen began providing stories to the local newspapers about his crooked policies. He died in 1923, and Amy appointed Leander Congos as the new marshal. Along with a helpful council, he was on board with her policies to remove bootlegging from the village. She licensed poolrooms and soft drink establishments, which allowed her to punish the saloons that were often hidden inside. Licenses weren't renewed or were revoked, and operators were heavily fined and sometimes sent to jail. She was one tough mayor and often even went on the raids of suspected bootlegging businesses herself.

She was also known for condemning corsets as "puritanical nonsense" and defending bobbed hair for women, short skirts, singing and dancing, once stating, "The cymbals, saxophone and violin make me move my feet."

Although many villagers were thrilled with the changes Kaukonen was making in their community, many were not happy. She received threats nearly every day of her term. Even before the election, gentlemen visited Kaukonen in her office, presenting her with a "block" of one-hundred-dollar bills to persuade her to quite the mayor's race.

During her term as mayor, she continued to work as the town's doctor, and became a popular spokesperson due to her hard political stance. She traveled to a number of cities to be honored at Anti-Saloon League meetings. President Warren G. Harding even gave her a letter of appreciation and a gift of two Airedale terrier dogs.

Kaukonen also declined a number of marriage proposals over her term but eventually married in 1928. She even donated her salary as mayor (fifty dollars a month) to the poor in her community.

In 1923, after serving two years as mayor, she abruptly resigned and moved to Seattle, Washington. One theory is that the threats, which seemed to get more drastic, pushed her to leave.

Mayor Amy Kaukonen and Marshal Leander Congos with materials confiscated from a bootlegger raid. *Courtesy of Lisa Potti.*

Although her term as mayor in Fairport was short, it came at a pivotal time when the village could have quickly declined. Instead, her fearlessness and tenacious spirit made her a leader of social change. She accomplished her goal of cleaning up the village and paved the way for its future success.

6

Agriculture and Industry

Hosea Brown Barn

The Hosea Brown Barn in Concord Township is the oldest documented barn in Lake County, built more than two centuries ago, in 1817.

A year earlier, Revolutionary War veteran Oliver Brown moved to the property from Connecticut with his wife Gracy and son Hosea (the barn's namesake). They built their house and barn using tall straight poplars hewn into posts and beams. According to Lake Metroparks, who now owns the property, as the family cleared the land, they hauled logs to a powered sawmill at nearby Big Creek to create boards and planks. Their barn was built in just twenty-nine days with three bays to house grain, hay and livestock. Two small, framed buildings were added to contain threshed out grain and dried corn on the cob.

In 1822, the same year the village separated from Painesville and became Concord, the Browns' daughter, Alva, was born. The family spent the next few decades on their working farm.

Then, in 1845, Hosea inherited the estate after Oliver died. In the 1850 census, Hosea listed four horses, seven milk cows and a team of oxen, and was raising thirty-five tons of hay, twenty bushels of wheat, fifty-five bushels of oats and one hundred bushels of corn.

The property was farmed into the early 1900s and passed through several generations. By the 1920s, it was showing signs of decline, and Hosea's

Hosea Brown Barn. *Photo by author.*

great-grandson Elijah H., then superintendent of Harding High School, was a great conservationist and set aside two hundred acres of the land for scouts and nature clubs.

Elijah was the last heir to the family farm when he died in the 1950s, so the property was put up for sale. Gladys and Arthur Buschmann bought it and ran it for years as a stock farm, raising beef cattle. After Gladys's death in 2002, Lake Metroparks purchased the Buschmann property, incorporating it into the nearby Girdled Road Reservation.

By this time, the barn had been altered many times and structural problems were evident, so it was deconstructed, old beams were repaired, new ones were hewn and it was reconstructed. In 2008, a construction firm erected the restored barn frame on its original foundation stones and site on the property.

Now the barn and land that the Brown family once farmed is preserved for future generations. Lake Metroparks even restored the fields with traditional grasses and added trails for all to enjoy the historic property.

FARMPARK

Lake Metroparks Farmpark in the rural setting of Kirtland is a popular place year-round for visitors attending programs or just enjoying the day on the expansive property. It's relatively new, having opened in 1990 as an outdoor education and cultural center, but the history of the property dates back nearly two centuries.

In 1831, Christopher G. Crary bought 156 acres of land from Joshua Stow of the Connecticut Land Company and nearly twenty years later purchased another 164 acres. He owned and farmed much of the property that is now Farmpark, raising cattle and sheep. (Crary Lane sits alongside the park.)

Then in 1882, Robert Criswell bought almost two-thirds of that land from Crary and grew fruit trees and grapes on the property for nearly fifty years. In the early 1940s, Grayce Farinacci bought the Criswell farm and eventually sold it to Dr. Leonard T. Skeggs and his wife, Jean Skeggs, who named the property Locust Farm in 1970.

Dr. Skeggs was a scientist, researcher and biochemist, born in Fremont in 1918. His family moved to Boardman when he was young, and he met and dated his wife-to-be in high school. He was proud to have served in the U.S. Navy during World War II and, after coming back from war, got his doctorate. In the 1950s, he invented the sequential blood analysis machine (SMA), which was a revolutionary way to automate blood analysis, and worked on a beta blocker high blood pressure pill. Companies originally didn't want to manufacture his blood analysis machines, but the Technicon Corporation eventually bought his design. Only fifty of his machines were sold in 1957, but by 1969, eighteen thousand machines were sold that year alone.

On July 4, 1968, a tornado tore through the region, causing extensive damage to trees on the farm. The Skeggs erected a temporary sawmill at Locust Farm and milled the wood from the damaged maple trees on nearby Blair Lane to use for the paneling in the exhibit hall and stables.

According to Skeggs's daughter, Dr. Laura Tradowsky, from 1970 to 1987, her parents bred Arabian horses on the farm. Laura says it all started with her own love of horses and led to her parents importing fifty-eight pure Polish Arabian horses from Poland over the years.

In 1987, Lake Metroparks bought the 235-acre farm from the Skeggs for $1.5 million, including existing barns, houses and an arena. Although one house near the well-bred shed was knocked down, another one remains on the property. The original house was destroyed by a fire in the early 1900s, and the Criswell barn burned down in July 1980, when lightning struck a two-story metal structure connected to the barn, which Dr. Skeggs created to house and dry alfalfa by blowing warm air up from the floor. The arena and well-bred shed were built by the Skeggs and, although they have been renovated, likely still contain some of the original timber.

After the Farmpark was created, Laura worked there as a food educator specialist for nearly a decade. Her father only visited a few times but loved to bake and won a Farmpark-sponsored muffin contest twice for his pumpkin pecan muffins. He died at the age of eighty-four in 2002.

A sculpted horse statue at the front walkway leading to the Farmpark visitor center is a symbol of the park's history. It's a bronze casting of Dr. Skeggs's Arabian stallion, Gwalior, who was a Reserve National Champion, and the horse's trainer, Gene LaCroix, sculpted by Laura's husband, Dr. Michael Tradowsky.

CARTER'S CORNERS

Connecticut Land Company shareholder Colonel Amasa Clapp of Massachusetts had drawn lots in township No. 10, range No. 7, in what is now Leroy Township. In 1802, he sent his sons, Elah and Paul, to clear six acres of this land, where they built a cabin and planted wheat fields that yielded fifteen to twenty bushels an acre the following year.

They paved the way for farmers like Samuel Carter, who, in 1870, was the wealthiest man in Leroy Township. He owned and farmed 440 acres of land that spanned all four corners of the intersection at Vrooman and Carter Roads, which became known as Carters Corners.

According to Lori Watson of the LeRoy Heritage Association (LHA), Samuel was the oldest son of Newcomb Carter, who traveled from Connecticut in 1835. It took Newcomb, his wife and four sons forty days to travel over the Allegheny Mountains and through Pittsburgh to Leroy. Samuel married Sophronia Clapp in 1837, and by 1840, the Carter family owned and started farming the land at Carters Corners.

Each year, they produced eighty tons of hay, 140 bushes of winter wheat, 600 bushels of Indian corn, 800 bushels of oats and 600 bushels of Irish potatoes. Samuel also owned dozens of horses, milk cows, sheep and swine. His sheep produced 150 pounds of wool, and he had a cheese factory on Vrooman Road, where he made 250 pounds of butter and 8,500 pounds of cheese.

On October 11, 1866, the *Painesville Telegraph* announced, "The Carter Brothers took the premium for Best Cheese at our County Fair. Their cheese is becoming celebrated all over the country." Later that month, the Carters were even awarded first premium on cheese at the Ohio State Fair. Then, in 1871, Samuel E. Carter & Co. made and exhibited a cheese weighing a whopping 1,100 pounds, at the Northern Ohio Fair.

At this point, Samuel was remarried to Emily Buel. (His first wife had died in 1851.) They lived in Leroy until 1882, moved to the Dakota Territory for more than a decade and returned to Leroy in 1894. Samuel died in 1896 in Madison at the home of his daughter W.F. Vrooman (one of his ten children, eight with his first wife and two with his second). He is buried at the Huntoon Cemetery in Concord.

The Carter land was divided many years ago, and private homes are scattered across much of it, including one where his potato fields once were and another at the site of the cheese factory. The Carter House still stands on the corner of Vrooman and Carter Roads and was said to have been built in 1850.

Perry Coal & Feed

Perry Coal & Feed has been in business on Main Street in Perry for over a century. It was founded by J.M. Brown in 1916, about a century after Perry Township was established and named for Oliver Hazard Perry, a U.S. naval officer who defeated a British squadron in the Battle of Lake Erie during the War of 1812.

It originally sold feed, fertilizer and flour. Later, investors bought the property and added a building to store milling equipment so they could actually make the feed on site, rather than buying and selling it.

Owner Rick Warren says at the time, everyone in Perry had a small family farm, so supplying feed was very important. The store still has a lot of the old equipment and can make feed on-site if needed. Warren also has a lot of other "really old stuff" up on the rafters in the mill, like big feed scoops and measuring scoops, some for a full bushel and others for a half. He says the scoops were used before feed was weighed, and made it easier to count bushels, depending on the number of scoops used.

Warren's store sits near the railroad tracks, and one of his buildings is actually an old railroad freight depot. On some of the original wood beams

Perry Coal & Feed. *Courtesy of Perry Coal & Feed.*

inside the building, he discovered the signatures of two men, perhaps the builders, dated October 1899. He thinks that was the year an addition was built because it has a basement underneath, with a cement floor, where they used to store onions (grown plentifully at the time throughout Perry) to keep them cool and crisp. The onions were then shipped by rail out of the region.

Warren also has what he believes is the original cash register used in the store until 1995, when it was replaced by computers. The solid brass register even survived a break-in when a burglar shoved it off the store safe trying to look for money. It remains an important remnant of the store's early history, made with a hand crank and numbers going up to $99.99, an amount that was probably rarely reached at the time.

Warren, who is the fifth generation on a Perry family farm, was hired by the store manager, his dad, Art, to work at Perry Coal and Feed when he was sixteen years old. Since then, he has seen the community change a lot. "When I started here it was very rural. Everyone still had a farm, and busiest days was always a Saturday because of weekend farmers," Rick said. Now, he says he can count on one hand the number of people who still do a little farming in the area, himself included.

Warren says fifty years ago, when he was a kid just starting out, busy stores surrounded Perry Coal & Feed, including Bailey Lumber, which used to be across the street, two grocery stores, a fire station, a mechanic garage/gun shop and a hardware store. Now, he says, his business is the only one left. In fact, Perry Coal & Feed might be the area's best kept secret.

Despite running his own farm with dozens of cattle and turkeys, and flying as a certified pilot (joking that he owns the back end of the plane because all of the expensive parts are in the front), he still goes the extra mile and puts his customers first using the same principles the store was founded on more than a century ago.

"I'm proud of it. There aren't a whole lot of businesses that make one hundred years," he said. "I can't contribute that to me or my dad. I attribute it to my customers. If we didn't have a customer base we wouldn't be here."

THE NURSERY BELT

Lake County has a defined nursery belt on its eastern side, about twenty miles wide, from Madison through west Mentor. It's about three to seven miles from north to south, beginning near the Lake Erie shoreline. Due to the proximity of the lake, the region stays warmer in the fall and is protected against early frosts.

Ease of transportation also contributed to the nursery belt's successful growing industry, when railroads and canals arrived in 1852, connecting local farmers to eastern markets.

All of this set the perfect stage for the hard-working people who are at the heart of making farms and nurseries pivotal. By the late 1930s, nursery sales provided about half of the county's income.

Storrs & Harrison Nursery

Jesse Storrs is credited with starting the nursery boom when he moved his family from Cortland, New York, and teamed up with English immigrant J.J. Harrison. They created the first landscape nursery—Storrs & Harrison Co.—in Painesville in 1854, and it became the largest departmental nursery in the world.

Their fields and facilities spanned both sides of Route 20, several miles east of downtown Painesville, all the way to Lake Erie. Workers arrived by train at the Nursery Stop, and their children were educated at the Nursery School (Hale Road Elementary School today).

Many employees hoped to open their own nurseries one day, so they wrapped cuttings from the plants they were tending each day and tucked them carefully into their lunch pails while also saving money to buy small plots. At one time, a section of homes between North Ridge Road and Madison Avenue was nicknamed "Lunchbox Nursery Row" because so many small nurseries got their start by being smuggled home in lunchboxes.

Wayside Gardens

Wayside Gardens opened as a roadside stand in 1916. When Elmer Schultz was eighteen years old, he started a three-acre nursery on Heisley Road. Wayside Gardens was officially formed in 1920, after he teamed up with co-owner J.J. Grullemans. In 1932, when headquarters moved to the historic Daniel Sawyer house on Mentor Avenue (at risk of being demolished at the time of this writing), Wayside grew to three hundred acres, spanning both sides of Heisley Road from Jackson Street to south of Mentor Avenue.

They believed in doing things the "right way," according to their 1930 catalog: "At times there's a lot of tall grumbling by our packers, about our being 'so doggone fussy' as they call it. However, plants so packed that 'doggone fussy' way, have a habit of getting to you in such condition, that when planted, they take right hold without any coddling. So we are going to keep on being fussy about the packing."

In 1945, when Schultz retired, Wayside Gardens was recognized as one of the largest nurseries in the world.

Gilson Gardens

Gilson Gardens was founded on North Ridge Road in Perry in 1947 on the former site of Werner Nursery. Paul Werner, a Polish immigrant, founded Werner's in 1920, growing lilies and perennials that he often sold to nearby Storrs & Harrison nursery.

The nursery was abandoned for several years after Werner tragically drowned while cooling off in Lake Erie. Eventually, Ted and Kathy Gilson

Edward S. Gilson. *Courtesy of his grandson Mark Gilson.*

and Ted's parents, Edward and Mildred, bought the nursery. Ted and Kathy moved from South Euclid to nearby Hale Road (nursery property owned by Storrs & Harrison in the early 1900s), and their parents moved into the nursery residence on North Ridge Road.

For years, Ted and Ed continued working their day jobs (Ted at Mentor Products and Ed at Bailey Meter) while running Gilson. They prepared cuttings in the morning before work and placed them in the greenhouse benches after they came back in the evening.

Mark Gilson, the most recent owner, shares his interest in local nursery history through articles and lectures and fondly remembers what it was like growing up in Perry: "We grew up thinking it normal that all our friends were nursery brats and that nurseries should dominate our local communities. Perry was a paradise for kids back then with hundreds of acres of overgrown nursery lands where we regularly escaped all parental supervision."

The Gilson family decided it was time to close Gilson Gardens in 2017, after a long and successful run.

Wyatt's Greenhouse

Wyatt's Greenhouse and Garden Center in Mentor started with the Wyatts' great-grandfather Cole. He was the original homesteader who farmed the property and sold produce from his horse-drawn wagon at the corner of Lakeshore Boulevard and Route 306.

The farm grew, and Wyatt's became known for its large variety of geraniums. Over a century later, Wyatt's is still family-run and known for its flowers, like the signature petunia hanging baskets. The original barns and family farmhouse still stand on the property.

MENTOR: THE ROSE CAPITAL OF THE NATION

Not only was Lake County once our country's nursery capital, but Mentor, nestled within that nursery belt, also held the title of Rose Capital of the Nation. At its peak, there were over a dozen large rose growers producing about five million plants a year.

Melvin E. Wyant

Roses once grew abundantly across from Mentor High School and throughout Civic Center Park. Rose specialist Melvin E. Wyant grew an extensive rose garden where a residential development now sits on Johnnycake Road, west of King Memorial. Wyant was a well-known commercial grower, rose judge and lecturer for more than fifty years. After graduating with a horticulture degree from The Ohio State University in 1918, he became a Lake County nursery inspector.

He decided "there weren't any [plants] as interesting, or as beautiful as the rose," so he bought five thousand rooted stock cuttings and planted them on rented land south of Painesville. He heard soil in Mentor was good for growing roses, so in 1925, he bought his first ten acres on a dirt road, Johnnycake Ridge. Over the next several decades, he cross-bred roses, developed hybrid tea roses and held patents on dozens of varieties.

Specialty roses in Storrs & Harrison catalogue. *Courtesy of Mark Gilson.*

Gerard K. Klyn

Gerard K. Klyn came to America in 1916 to sell products from his father's nursery in Holland but wasn't able to return home until World War I ended. He came back to the United States in 1921 to plant his first rose cuttings and establish the Gerard K. Klyn Inc. Nursery in Mentor. It started with just five acres and grew to 450 on Jackson Street and Hopkins Road, with many cuttings imported from the family nursery in Holland.

Klyn's Garden Center postcard, late 1950s. *Courtesy of Bill Smith.*

In 1957, Klyn's Garden Center opened on Route 20, west of Mentor, and by 1958, Klyn was said to be the largest rose grower in the Midwest. After Klyn passed away in the 1960s, the nursery moved to Perry, although it no longer grows roses, it produces over 1,600 plant varieties a year.

Today, one of the only remnants of this once-booming industry is the Commemorative Rose Garden on Mentor Avenue, complete with a historical plaque, and nearby streets with rose-related names, such as Tea Rose, Wyant and Rosebud Drives.

DEBONNE VINEYARDS

Nestled in the valley of the Grand River, along the southern shore of Lake Erie, sits Lake County's wine region. This section of land is home to well over half of the wine grape acreage in Ohio. It draws tens of thousands of visitors to the county each year.

The award-winning Debonne Vineyards in Madison Township has been a popular place to visit for decades. It's run by the Debevc family, and their property includes 160 acres of vines, making it the largest estate winery in Ohio. Although they make and sell many wine varieties, as well as beer, they are best known for their Riesling.

Wine making goes back far in the Debevc family. It started more than a century ago, when Anton Debevc and his family first moved to Madison Township. He immigrated to the area from the Slovenian state of Yugoslavia, where he had a lumber mill, in 1914 and purchased a farm in Madison in 1916. (The region, settled in 1802, was first called Chapintown, named after an early settler, then later Centerville and it became known as Madison Township by 1811, named after President James Madison.)

Anton farmed everything, raised chickens and pigs, had several dairy cows and grew peaches, pears, apples and grapes. He had always made wine and even had a still, since it was just before Prohibition. The Debevcs had three daughters and a son, Tony. Since he was the only boy, he stopped going to school in eighth grade to help on the farm and, years later, bought the adjacent property to the farm, where there was a vineyard.

Grandson Tony Jr. graduated from The Ohio State University with a degree in horticulture in 1969. In 1971, after two years as an army paratrooper, he came back to Madison. He had his pilot's license and was initially more interested in pursuing a career as a pilot instead of as a winemaker, but flying jobs were scarce as pilots returned from Vietnam. So, he bought fifty-five acres, where the winery sits today, from a lady who had a little dairy. Since they've always made wine, he thought, why not open a winery?

Tony and his wife, Beth Debevc, currently own Debonne Vineyards. According to Beth, "My husband had the vision and wanted to make the wine, my father-in-law had the land, and Rose, my mother-in-law did the paperwork."

So, Tony Sr. and Tony Jr. built a chalet to house the winery, opened to the public in 1972, and figured if it didn't work out, they could always live there. "It was very successful immediately. There was no question that we weren't going to make it," says Beth. "There were years there was a frost where we lost a bunch of grapes. So, we made something else."

Beth and Tony met in 1972, got married in 1975 and they've been running the winery since, now with their son Tony (known by many at the winery simply as "Junior"). Until Tony Sr.'s death in 2010, he was also involved with the winery by acting as vineyard manager emeritus. The Chairman's White wine that they produce is also a tribute to the founder of the winery.

The Debevcs continue to expand their business and recently opened another winery in Madison called Cask 307. Thanks to Michael Harris, their wine maker, they've come a long way from their earliest days, when they were still selling Concord grapes to Coca-Cola. In their first year, they

Chalet Debonne original building. *Courtesy of Beth Debevc.*

produced 5,000 gallons of wine, with a goal of making 20,000 gallons. Today they are producing 130,000 gallons.

According to Beth, it was the first winery to open in the Western Reserve area since Prohibition. It paved the way for other wineries to follow in its footsteps. Grand River Cellars (known at the time as the Grand River Winey Company) opened next, in 1976, and by the 1980s, there was a winery boom in Madison and Grand River that has continued to this day.

The Debevc family still lives in the original home that was located on Anton's farm, with a century home plaque on the front. The house, built by Anton's son, Tony, is currently operating as an Airbnb rental. They are preserving their family's history while continuing to meet the needs of the evolving wine industry.

SHAKER VINEYARDS LAND COMPANY

Worden Road in Wickliffe was named after Worden Blue grapes at a time when vineyards covered more than one thousand acres of land in the surrounding region. From the 1890s to the early 1900s, the grape-growing business was one of the largest in Wickliffe (named after Postmaster General Charles Anderson Wickliffe).

In 1892, Elder Joseph Slingerland, head trustee of the Western Shakers, a religious sect known as the United Society of Believers in Christ's Second Coming, came to Wickliffe. The land along Lake Erie, below Ridge Road, was considered some of the finest in the country at the time, and the growing season was extended a little longer, thanks to warm breezes from the lake and a delayed frost.

Slingerland bought property and created the Shaker Vineyards Land Company. He bought three hundred acres from William Lloyd (namesake of Lloyd Road) and asked him to start planting vineyards for him. He bought another seven hundred acres from the adjoining Wilson Farm, along with other small parcels of land.

The vineyards, mainly between Worden and Lloyd Roads, were in a prime location because the S. Louis (Nickel Plate) and Lake Shore Michigan Southern (LS&MS) railroads ran through the area, making shipping accessible.

The newly planted vineyards took several years to grow, and grape harvesting began in 1897, using special wooden baskets with light wooden covers designed specifically for both packaging and shipping grapes. Four carloads of grapes were shipped daily during the season, containing 2,700 baskets per shipment.

Although the Shakers were benefitting financially, they weren't living in the community. The venture only lasted about a decade and was abandoned by the Shakers after a severe frost and the death of William Lloyd, who oversaw the vineyards.

Remnants of the vineyards exist today in the names of area roads, including Shaker Drive, Vineyard Drive and Vineyard Road in Willowick, along with streets named after grapes, such as Catawba Street and Delaware Street. Even today, wild grape plants are sometimes found throughout the area, climbing up trees in backyards or growing on fences along the freeway.

There were also private picnic grounds and a pavilion at the corner of Grand Boulevard and Worden Road in the 1920s. It was known as Camp Heck. The Worden Road Mini Mart, located across the street on Worden Road, is believed to have originally been a pumphouse for the neighborhood in the 1930s, perhaps connected with Camp Heck or the homes that began popping up nearby.

MOUNTAIN CREEK TREE FARM

For many Lake County residents, grabbing a saw and sled and hiking out into rows of pine trees searching for the perfect Christmas tree to cut down is a family tradition. Like other areas of agriculture, Christmas tree farms have found success in Lake County, thanks to the climate and soil. Although there are other tree farms, Mountain Creek Tree Farm on Williams Road in Concord Township is the oldest.

The history of the fifty-two-acre tree farm dates much further back than when the first official Christmas tree was sold in 1956. According, to owner Ken Reeves, who took over running the farm from his parents about a decade ago, his great uncle Orlin Goudy bought the property in the 1920s, when it was a working farm.

The house on the property was built as a small cabin in 1836. It has been added to over the years, just like the barn that predates it, according to historical documents the Reeves found while researching and gathering documents to attain the house's historical plaque. This follows a pattern that was common in the early days when pioneers settled the area, likely taking nearby Girdled Road into the Western Reserve. They generally built a barn first to house their animals and livelihood and then built their homes.

Mountain Creek Tree Farm's historic red barn. *Photo by author.*

Inside the original barn at Mountain Creek Tree Farm. *Photo by author.*

In the late 1940s, Goudy got the idea from a business associate to plant one thousand scotch pine trees and start a Christmas tree farm. Before World War II, it was common practice to trek through the woods, even state and national forests, to cut down a Christmas tree. After the war, the population was increasing to a point that the federal government began restricting people from cutting down trees in the woods, giving many, like Goudy, with an entrepreneurial spirit the chance to start their own tree farms. Although some tree farms started popping up in the 1940s, according to Reeves, most didn't start until the '60s and '70s.

When the business first began, it was slow-going because I-90 didn't exist, and customers had fewer options to travel to the farm. Today, the tree farm is bustling in the weeks leading up to Christmas.

According to Reeves, many families (mine included) have been coming to the tree farm for years. Last year, a woman even brought her father, a World War II veteran who wanted to see the farm because he brought his family there to cut down their tree dating to the 1950s.

"I truly, truly enjoy those stories and just being able to be a part of so many families' Christmases over the years," Reeves explained. "That's really special."

Fairport Morton Salt Mine

People have been using salt, also sometimes called white gold, for thousands of years. Although Morton Salt started in Chicago during the gold rush in the 1800s, the company drilled the mines in Fairport in 1959. This became one of the country's deepest salt mines of the time.

Locals can see mounds of salt at Morton Salt in Fairport from various vantage points, including the entrance to Mentor Headlands State Park. However, the mines themselves that lie two thousand feet under Lake Erie are a hidden mystery to many. They are made of dark corridors and tunnels weaving through salt deposits that are the dried remains of a four-hundred-million-year-old inland sea.

The mine's main work site actually sits about three miles out into the lake. To get there, workers ride down on an elevator and then take gas-powered golf carts even deeper into a long, dark, salt-encrusted tunnel. Enormous machines are used for drilling, extracting and crushing huge chunks of salt so that it can fit in buckets that are then brought back to the surface on conveyors.

Morton produces about 1.3 million tons of salt each year, mainly used to deice roadways.

Willoughby's First Traffic Signal

Clevelander Garret Morgan Sr. was a Black inventor and businessman who blazed a trail with his many inventions. In 1922, he invented the traffic light and first tested it out at a busy intersection in downtown Willougbhy at Erie and Vine Streets.

At the time, drivers had only green and red signals, which were manually operated and stopped abruptly, so the design was much different from today's version. Morgan was the first to add a third signal, for caution, which helped make driving safer by providing extra reaction time before a stop. The signal Morgan patented was a T-shaped pole with a three-position traffic signal. The signal had three arms—one to stop traffic in one direction, one to go and a third to stop traffic in all directions. The U.S. Patent and Trademark Office refers to it as the forerunner of modern traffic lights.

In 2011, students from the Willoughby Tech Center welding class created a replica of the traffic light that stands on Vine Street, near the original test location.

7

SCHOOLS AND EDUCATION

OLD STONE SCHOOLHOUSE

The Old Stone Schoolhouse on Ravenna Road in Concord Township is just one of several remaining one-room schoolhouses in Lake County. Built in 1840, at a cost of $200, it's one of the oldest structures in the township and was one of nine one-room schoolhouses in Concord School District, with students attending from 1841 to 1923.

In 2001, Concord Township purchased the property, restored it and opened it as the township museum and historical society in 2006. Thanks to the efforts of the township and a group of volunteers known as Friends of the Old Stone Schoolhouse, more people are learning about the schoolhouse's history.

Dan Maxson, docent and curator for the Old Stone Schoolhouse, graciously showed me around the historic building. It houses artifacts and stories of local history, along with several original pieces, like the school construction contract dated November 23, 1840; student diaries; bells; books; and ledgers. Some items were left inside over the years while others were uncovered in the basement (always a good hiding place for historic treasures) of town hall or in the community center or were donated by the community. (Maxson and co-author Debra Bechel-Esker are compiling intriguing history, including that of the schoolhouse, for their Arcadia Publishing book, *Concord: The First 200 Years*, to coincide with Concord's bicentennial.)

Above: Old Stone Schoolhouse. *Photo by author.*

Right: Marian Leuty in her Women's Army Corps (WAC) uniform. *Photo by author.*

When visiting the one-room schoolhouse, it's clear that rules of teaching have drastically changed in the past century. Not only are students now taught by grade instead of in one single room, but rules of conduct are also much different.

Teachers' rules of 1915 offer a glimpse of the stringent life they were expected to live:

> *You will not marry during the term of your contract.*
> *You are not to keep company with men.*
> *You must be home between the hours of 8 p.m. and 6 a.m. unless*
>   *attending a school function.*
> *You may not loiter downtown in ice cream stores.*
> *You may not dress in bright colors.*
> *You may, under no circumstances, dye your hair.*

According to rules of conduct in 1872, "Men teachers may take one evening each week for courting purposes, or two evenings a week if they go to church regularly."

One section is dedicated to former student Marian Leuty, who later became an elementary school teacher in Concord. She was in the Women's Army Corps (WAC) in World War II, and a photo of her in uniform is proudly displayed, along with the American flag presented to her family after her death. Visitors can see her diary, along with a reproduction of a letter she wrote on September 24, 1919, when she was a student.

It reads like a written time capsule:

> *Dear Friend in the Far-Away Future,*
>
>   *My teacher, Miss Topper, said I should write you a letter. We are to write to someone in the future and tell him or her about our lives.*
>
>   *My name is Marian. I am a 13-year-old girl, and I go to a one-room schoolhouse in Concord, Ohio. There are eight grades and twenty-five pupils all being taught in the same room. I walk a half-mile to school every morning during the fall, winter, and spring. Miss topper teachers Arithmetic, Physiology, History, Grammar, Gym, Music, Spelling, and Geography.*
>
>   *I wear my serge dress to school every day. My mother just put a new silk front on it. I change clothes when I get home, so I won't rip or dirty my dress when I do chores. During the winter, I wear long, itchy, white underwear under my dress. It feels so good when summer comes and I can wear lighter clothes. I like to go barefoot in the summer.*

I have long, curly hair and I don't like it when my mother combs it. She tugs hard at the snarls and it hurts. I tie a big bow in my hair after she is finished combing it. I wash and starch my hair ribbons once a week. I iron the ribbons with the heavy iron that we heat on the top of our stove.

I have to help with the housework when I get home from school. On Mondays, my mother and I do the laundry. My mother boils towels, white clothes and Fels Naphtha [sic] soup in a copper boil on top of the wood-burning stove. After the clothes are boiled, she lifts them out with a big paddle and puts them into our wooden washing machine. She adds bluing to the wash water to make the clothes white. There is a stick attached to the washing machine which activates a paddle inside. It is my job the push the stick back and forth to agitate the clothes. I do this for ten minutes and it is hard work. I sing a song with a strong beat as I thump the stick back and forth. We wash at least three loads of clothes; the white clothes first, colored clothes next and the men's overalls, shirts and socks last. By the last load, the water is black!

I help my mother hang the clothes outside. I like this best during the summertime. I enjoy seeing the clean clothes on the line in the sunshine. In wintertime, we hang the clothes out to freeze dry and bring them into the kitchen to thaw by the stove.

I help my mother with the cooking. One time, I was naughty and took a small lump of brown sugar out of the pantry and ate it. Much to my surprise, it wasn't brown sugar, but a chunk of hot, dry mustard! I never did that again.

For fun, my friends Adelaide, Charlotte, and I like to pick wildflowers. On May 1st, we wove baskets out of construction paper and filled them with flowers. We hung them on our neighbor's front door, knocked on the door and ran. What a nice surprise for the neighbors!

Today we heard an aeroplane fly over the school. We all ran out to see it. The teacher told us two Ohio men, Orville and Wilbur Wright, invented aeroplanes sixteen years ago.

This is my last year at the Stone Schoolhouse. Next year my aunt and I will rent a room in town, so I can go to Harvey High School without walking the four miles to Painesville every morning.

I hope you have enjoyed hearing about my life. I wonder what your life is like. Do you enjoy picking wildflowers too?

Love, Marian

After the schoolhouse closed, it was used as a business office and private residence. In the 1960s, it was the site manager's house when I-90 was built nearby. In the 1980s, local builder Bob Moore used it as his construction company's office. (Moore and his wife, Rose, later became instrumental in renovating the aging building.)

Elga Radcliffe Pomeroy spent much of her life in the Old Stone Schoolhouse, first as a student around 1910 and then years later as a teacher and in her senior years as a resident. At the time, she became a founding member of the Concord Garden Club, begun in the 1960s, and she lovingly tended to her roses and gardens on the ground. Pomeroy lived in the schoolhouse until she died at the age of 105 in 1987. A beautiful antique clock that belonged to her while she lived in the schoolhouse has recently been donated back and is on display. (Locals might recognize her maiden name, Radcliffe, as a nearby street bears the name.)

Other historic treasures can be found outside of the building, including what is believed to be the original bell (at least in part), a cement slab that was part of a hitching post (used to get on and off a horse) and a horse trough, recently moved from the fire station, with "1909" etched into the side, wearing away from weather and time. It is firsthand evidence of why it's so important to restore treasures like this schoolhouse and surrounding property so that it can be preserved before it fades away.

WILLOUGHBY UNIVERSITY OF LAKE ERIE

In 1834, settlers Dr. George Card and Dr. John Henderson decided to start a medical school in Chagrin. Willoughby University of Lake Erie was established as the first medical college in northeast Ohio, named after Dr. Westell Willoughby of Fairfield College, New York, whom they admired. They asked him to become president of their new school, but Willoughby declined. He did help develop the school from afar by choosing professional staff, selecting equipment, developing curriculum and donating $1,200.

The college suffered financial difficulties from the beginning but took a big hit in the 1840s, when faculty were accused of grave robbing to obtain bodies for dissection and teaching purposes. During this tumultuous time, when mobs of appalled residents regularly stormed the school, faculty members left to become affiliated with schools that were forerunners of the

School of Medicine of Case Western Reserve University and the Starling Medical College of the Ohio State University.

Willoughby University was the first medical college in the United States to be named after a person instead of a geographic location. And its creation led to a new name for the region—Willoughby. It was named for a man who influenced the school but never set foot in the town that was named after him.

LAKE ERIE COLLEGE

Lake Erie College in Painesville got its start as the Willoughby Female Seminary in 1847. Housed in the former Willoughby University of Lake Erie building, it was the only institution in the Western Reserve where women could get a higher education. It was known as Mount Holyoke College's "first godchild of the West." (Mount Holyoke Female Seminary opened in Massachusetts in 1837 and became a model for women's colleges.)

One morning in 1854, the building caught on fire and burned to the ground. It was rebuilt fifteen miles to the east, in Painesville, and opened as the Lake Erie Female Seminary (now Lake Erie College.)

College Hall

The Lake Erie Female Seminary officially incorporated in 1856, and the first cornerstone was laid for College Hall a year later. A *Painesville Telegraph* article printed after the occasion reads: "It is quite a modern idea, this, that Girls are capable of any considerable intellectual improvement.…In this Lake Erie Seminary it is proposed to give young ladies the opportunity for securing as good an education in every way, as the best colleges of the land are furnishing young men."

College Hall, designed by Jonathan Goldsmith's son-in-law Charles Wallace Heard, is 180 feet wide, like the White House, and 60 feet deep, like the Mormon Temple in Kirtland (before College Hall's south wing was added later). From the beginning, the community was involved. Men helped with construction and landscaping, and women held sewing circles to make bedding, table linens and draperies for the new building.

As students enrolled, the healthiest girls were assigned boarding rooms on the third floor, since they were able to climb the long flights of steps. Perhaps

College Hall at Lake Erie College. *Photo by author.*

Postcard of Lake Erie College entrance, 1910. *Author's collection.*

it was some of these agile climbers who led to a change in the college's facade. The campus was originally fronted by a white wooden fence with a flat rail on top, but this was replaced in 1893 by a wrought iron fence because the previous rail was too tempting to a number of girls who regularly enjoyed walking along the top.

Notable Visitors

Many famous people visited the college over the years, including President Abraham Lincoln, who spoke on the steps of College Hall. Famous aviatrix Amelia Earhart spoke to its Aviators Club in 1939, when the Civil Aeronautics Authority approved Lake Erie College for a civilian pilot program. President James A. Garfield celebrated what turned out to be his last birthday at the college. According to Deb Remington, director of alumni relations at Lake Erie College, the students presented President Garfield with a needlepoint for his birthday, and it is hanging over his summer bed in his home on Mentor Avenue.

President Garfield's wife, Lucretia, was in a women's circle at the college, while their son Abram helped build part of the college, and their grandson James Garfield was on the board for decades.

Matthews House

The campus is filled with fascinating buildings like the Matthews House, currently housing alumni and community relations and used as a guest house for esteemed visitors. It was designed by Jonathan Goldsmith in 1829 for his friend Dr. John Henry Matthews, who delivered one of the Goldsmith babies in 1812.

Dr. Mathews was married to Martha Devotion Huntington, daughter of Ohio's third governor, and they had four children, including Samuel Huntington, who attended the Willoughby Medical College and lived in the home for years. After the seminary opened, the college asked Samuel Huntington's second wife, Maria Dean Matthews, to open a preparatory school for young ladies. So, she added a room to the back of her house and opened her school in the 1870s, training more than 350 young women over a twenty-five-year period.

In 1951, the college bought the home, saving it from being razed for a car dealership. It was moved from North State Street to West Washington Street in three parts. The parlors were moved separately and reattached, and Mrs. Matthews continued to live in the home for the rest of her life.

A few pieces of original furniture remain in the house, along with Dr. Matthews's cane and his portrait. Some even say the doctor still visits; the Matthews House is just one of many buildings on Lake Erie College campus that is believed to be haunted. According to Remington, she heard an account from a guest who once stayed overnight, saying they heard a cane hitting the floor and believed it was Dr. Matthews.

Steele Mansion

In the mid-1800s, the Steele Mansion, built for George Steele, was described in a newspaper as the "grandest home in Painesville." It was built with a third-floor ballroom, eight Italian marble fireplaces, windows imported from France and three bathrooms with running water. The Steele family lived in the front of the home, while servants lived in the two-story rear wing, until the early 1900s, when it was sold to Lake Erie College. For decades, the college used it as the president's home, student housing and administrative offices. The ballroom was once used as a gymnasium. In the 1970s, it was sold to a private owner who converted it into apartments, and it suffered devastating damages (including the loss of the third floor and roof) during a fire in 2001.

It sat open to the elements for nearly a decade before it was rescued from near demolition and has been restored to its original grandeur. It has found new life as a historic inn and meeting center and even has a suite named after Amelia Earhart, who once stayed there.

Helen Rockwell Morley Memorial Music Building

In the late 1950s, the college acquired the five-hundred-acre Morley Farm after being named principal benefactor in the will Charles R. Morley, a thirty-seven-year college trustee.

The farm, located in the coveted Little Mountain region, included a twenty-three-room Manor House and attached library and art gallery, a three-acre lake, two tenant houses, three barns and other buildings. Morley

Helen Rockwell Morley Music Hall at Lake Erie College. *Photo by author.*

Road was constructed to transport family members and guests from the train or trolley to the farm.

It was the summer home of Jesse Healy Morley and his third wife, Helen Rockwell Morley, graduate of Willoughby Seminary and daughter of one of Lake Erie's founders.

By 1912, the farmhouse had doubled in size, and nearly a decade later, Charles began adding a library wing, designed by J. Milton Dyer. He built the exterior from stone dug up on the property's three quarries to create a fireproof treasury for his books and paintings.

Since Mrs. Morley and her son Charles were living there alone, she approached the college to see if there was an educated young woman who could step in as her travel companion, which was very common at the time. Lake Erie College recommended Hildegard, a teacher of French and English literature. Charles and Hildegard fell in love, but his mother did not approve. According to Remington, when Mrs. Morley died, the two got married, and in the late 1920s, Charles built the $300,000 Rockwell Morley Music Building in honor of his mother, hoping to appease her spirit. In fact, that's why the colors inside were pink and turquoise—her favorite colors.

Her spirit is believed to torment people as they practice piano in the hall by screaming and knocking the music sheets off the piano.

The building, considered acoustically one of the best small concert halls in the world, houses both a 1925 Steinway grand piano and 1927 E.M. Skinner organ. The building is regularly used by students and even served as the site for Ohio Supreme Court's sessions in the 1970s.

CHILDREN'S SCHOOLHOUSE NATURE PARK

A bell is ringing in the tower of a historic one-room schoolhouse on the corner of Booth and Baldwin Roads. Children rush out the door and down the steps after wrapping up special nature programs, just as they did more than a century ago, trying to catch a glimpse of the still-ringing bell before heading back home. It's the same bell, albeit several times repaired, that rang at the top of the schoolhouse when it was a functioning full-time school.

The building dates to 1854, when the Kirtland Township Board of Education bought a quarter-acre of land in Lot 10, Tract 1 from Hiram P. Harmon. According to Kirsten Bell, interpretive manager at the Lake Metroparks Children's Schoolhouse Nature Park, the land actually belonged to Hiram's half-sister, Sarah Harmon. She inherited it from her father, Oliver Harmon Jr., of Kirtland, who left "a schedule of property" to support his widow, Lucy Harmon, and his minor child, Sarah. Because Sarah was still a minor, Hiram was appointed as guardian for the sale of property. A frame building was built on the East Branch of the Chagrin River and referred to as the Chair Factory School, because a chair factory was located nearby.

Since a fire destroyed early records of the Kirtland Board of Education, some information can't be verified, but according to an unconfirmed story, at one point, the original schoolhouse was swept away by the creek on the property, which is hard to imagine, considering the low water level of the creek today. The current building on the site was rebuilt and opened as Riverside School or Riverside School No. 2 in 1894, which places it in school district two of nine in Kirtland Township at that time.

According to a class photo from 1895, courtesy of Lake Metroparks, there were more than forty students at the one-room schoolhouse that year, and the teacher's name was Genie L. Pomeroy. The class had a motto, "Read and you will know," and even its own class flower, a rose.

Left: Lake Metroparks Children's Schoolhouse Nature Park. *Photo by author.*

Below: The 1895 class at Riverside School (present-day Children's Schoolhouse Nature Park). *Courtesy of Lake Metroparks.*

Glenetta Booth Bar was a student at Riverside School in 1906 and 1907 and returned to teach in 1921 and 1922. Lake Metroparks has preserved a poem she wrote capturing what Christmas was like at the schoolhouse, but it's unclear if it was written when she was a student or teacher.

Christmas at Riverside School
by Glenetta Booth Bar

O, come with me to Kirtland Hills
To the Vale of Make-Believe,
And we'll celebrate together
One more joyous Christmas Eve.

Across the fields and woodlands
The snow lies deep and white,
And isn't it fun to ride
In this quaint old sleigh tonight?

We can hear the school bell ringing
In tones so crisp and clear,
Urging us to hasten
As we come from far and near.

And through the open doorway
A welcome light is streaming,
And from their brackets on the wall
The burnished lamps are gleaming.

The room is decked with hemlock
There are branches everywhere,
'Tis the symbol of the Yuletide
And its fragrance fills the air.

Here we stand in breathless wonder
As we gaze upon the tree.
Tappers, treats and trimmings,
And all for you and me.

We say our precious pieces,
And we hear sweet Gladys play,
And we sing the grand old carols
In the old familiar way.

Former student Florence Sheffield shared her experience at the schoolhouse with Leta D. Cardwell for Leta's 1972 dissertation. Sheffield said everyone looked forward to the Christmas program with great anticipation: "All the families would arrive in their sleighs with bells on. The children had made popcorn strings, cranberry strings and colored paper chains to put on the school tree. Alex Booth would come the day before the program and draw a Christmas scene on the blackboard with colored chalk."

Sheffield said one of the students would play Santa, and after all of the poems and recitations were heard, the little candles, clipped on the branches of the trees, were lit. "Then Santa would pass out boxes of popcorn for each child. One year Santa backed into the lit tree. His suit caught on fire. Several of the men present ran outside and grabbed the water bucket. It had ice on the surface but was sufficient to put out Santa. A whole box of crayons just for myself made them very special, and brings back memories of a long remembered fragrance."

By 1877, school attendance was required by law, and by 1900, grading became compulsory, and more one-room schoolhouses began consolidating with modern school districts. In 1921, the schoolhouse officially closed. In 1923, the schoolhouse and one-quarter acre of land was integrated into the surrounding estate of Leonard C. Hanna Jr., who owned Hilo Farms. By 1927, all eight of the one-room schoolhouses of Kirtland were consolidated into the Kirtland Township School District, and classes were held at the Kirtland High School Annex.

The newly formed Village of Kirtland Hills began using the schoolhouse as its village hall and continued until the present hall was built in 1952.

For more than a decade, the schoolhouse remained vacant. Then in 1963, three hundred acres of the Hanna Estate, including the schoolhouse, was purchased by a developer, and a subdivision property was created, called Hilo Farms (named after Hanna's original property). A year later, Anthony C. Ocepek and his family bought the schoolhouse, along with almost six acres of Hilo Farms land, and converted it into their family home.

They happily lived there for many years, raising their children on the property. Then in 1988, the Ocepek family donated the schoolhouse and twelve acres of surrounding land to Lake Metroparks for the development of a children's environmental education program.

Anthony Ocepek said the schoolhouse was a special place for his family, and they wanted children to again be the focus of programs offered there. "I am extremely partial to the outdoors, growing up in the country, having the opportunity to roam the woods. Mark, Beth, and Paul [the Ocepeks' children] had the same experience. We wanted to make sure the experience would carry on and that the building would never be destroyed. So the Metroparks, with their leadership, their ability, and their philosophy was the perfect place for the schoolhouse."

According to Lake Metroparks, Ocepek was inspired by Warren Corning, a philanthropist who was instrumental in developing the Holden Arboretum, donating the Lantern Court Estate. Ocepek said, "We would go for a walk about once a month. And one of the things he told me, which I will never forget, and I'll impart to other people; 'If you ever have the ability to give something, give it during your lifetime so that you can see it done right and enjoy it.'"

Lake Metroparks began a fundraising campaign for the development of a children's nature park. In 1990, Robert Bateman, an internationally known wildlife artist, heard about the project from local art dealers, Alan and Norah Lynne Brown, owners of Gallery One in Mentor. Bateman then raised $32,500 for the project.

In 1992, Lake Metroparks Children's Schoolhouse Nature Park officially opened, and since then, children and adults have been enjoying programs focused on Lake County's natural heritage through the three *R*s of environmental education: respect, responsibility and reverence.

Balch House

In 1802, pioneers started settling in Chesterfield, which is now Leroy Township (named after LeRoy, New York). According to Lori Watson, treasurer and historian of the LeRoy Heritage Association, the post office required the spelling to later change to Leroy because a town spelled LeRoy already existed in Medina County. However, Watson's family has been in Leroy since 1817, and they continue to pronounce it "la roy."

At one point in the 1800s, northeast LeRoy was its own little settlement, according to Watson, and it included many immigrants from the Isle of Man. There was a church on one corner and a schoolhouse on the other.

The Balch house on Trask Road sat across the street from the school and was built around 1860 by Charles Milo Balch. His father, Charles Balch Sr., was born in Chittenden, Virginia, in 1809 and traveled to Ohio to purchase the property at the corner of Ford and Trask in 1835. He

Northeast LeRoy Methodist Church with Schoolhouse No. 3 across the street. *Courtesy of LeRoy Heritage Association.*

had married Electa Covey in 1838, in Thompson, and his home had sat four hundred feet behind the home that his son would eventually build. (His brother, Joel Balch, also owned land on the corner, according to the 1857 map.)

The home built by Charles M. Balch sat on a farm that, in 1870, produced 80 bushels of wheat, 100 bushels of corn and 160 bushels of oats. It was also a post office at one point.

According to *History of Leroy*, second edition, the Balch family then sold land to Leroy Township for twenty dollars, stipulating that a church be built on the property. So, sometime before 1860, the Methodist church was built and sat diagonally across from the Balch house on Ford Road. Some of its earliest members were women who were "industrious and frugal to a remarkable degree, and helped make the neighborhood one of the most prosperous in the town," according to the *Memorial to the Pioneer Women of the Western Reserve*, of 1896.

According to Watson, sometime after 1930, LeRoy Schoolhouse No. 3, located across the street in front of the cemetery, was moved and added to the church to create a larger school, and the cemetery was then expanded. The schoolhouse then included a cloak room and two classrooms—one for grades first through fourth and another for grades fifth through eighth. The schoolhouse also had a bell that was known to "jump the cradle" if the rope was pulled too hard.

The schoolhouse, which was pivotal to the development of the community over the years, was sold to private owners in 1945, and still remains today.

LITTLE RED SCHOOLHOUSE

On a snowy winter day in Willoughby Township in the early 1900s, Anna Dowling could be found busily filling the pot belly stove with wood to keep her students warm. She rode the streetcar from Painesville into Willoughby Township each day to teach her students in grades one through eight, to make hot cocoa for their lunches, wade through the snow to flag down the interurban train for them to ride home at the end of the day and even to clean the schoolhouse.

Miss Dowling, as the students called her, graduated from Painesville High School and began teaching in 1908 at the age of seventeen. She got her start at the Brakeman School in LeRoy Township and two years later began teaching at District No. 7 in Willoughby Township, known today as the Little Red Schoolhouse.

The Little Red Schoolhouse was built in 1901 and was designed to hold about thirty students, in eight grades. Willoughby Township was divided into thirteen two-mile radius districts spanning several cities, since they were

A class from Harvey Hall District No. 7 (presently the Little Red Schoolhouse) with teacher Miss Anna Dowling. *Courtesy of Little Red Schoolhouse.*

all part of Willoughby Township at the time. Several of the other original Willoughby Township schoolhouses still exist and are privately owned, including one on Euclid Avenue and another on Reeves Road.

Today the Little Red Schoolhouse is on Shankland Road in Willoughby, just down the street from South High School, but the District No. 7 schoolhouse was originally located on Euclid Avenue near Campbell Road, by the Willowick border. Most children walked to school, but those who were lucky enough rode a horse and hitched it outside the schoolhouse or even rode on the interurban.

According to the minutes of a board of education meeting in 1916, Dowling was paid $75 a month, with an additional $5 for her duties as school janitor. By 1920, she was making $1,350 a year, with an additional $15 per month for car fare.

While teaching, Dowling continued to take courses in the summer at Western Reserve University and evening classes at Kent State University and Lake Erie College. By 1923, her hard work paid off, and Dowling was appointed the principal of Roosevelt School at East 322nd and Vine Street in Willowick, which had just been built a year earlier.

Possibly due to the stringent rules teachers had to follow at the time, including very little socializing outside of the classroom, Dowling never married. She dedicated forty-five years of her life to the Willoughby Township school district and made an impact on the lives of countless children.

Many of her memories and those of her students were compiled in a book published in 1978 and written by then Little Red Schoolhouse director, Eleanor Gaines Rolf. It is called *Willoughby Township Schools: The First One Hundred Years*.

Dowling said that although teaching methods changed throughout her career, she found the best way to reach a child was through kindness and patience. She died in 1976, a year after attending a Little Red Schoolhouse reunion with a number of her former students.

The Little Red Schoolhouse was a school for twenty-four years and was then used for storage for about fifty years by a succession of owners. In the mid-1970s, a group of residents began a campaign to save the historic schoolhouse, as it sat vacant on Euclid Avenue. They persuaded the Willoughby-Eastlake Board of Education to donate land on Shankland Road.

It became known as the Little Red Schoolhouse Project, and the goal was to move the schoolhouse in time for the city's bicentennial celebration. So, in late November 1975, while the Willoughby Bicentennial Committee was

Little Red Schoolhouse at original location on Euclid Avenue. *Courtesy of Little Red Schoolhouse.*

still trying to raise the $25,000 to cover the cost of the move and restoration, the schoolhouse was transported down Euclid Avenue and up Shankland to its present site.

The hope was to preserve the schoolhouse to show what it was like at its prime and to teach visitors, especially children, disappearing crafts like candle making, spinning and weaving.

Today, Cathi Weber is the director of the Little Red Schoolhouse, and she is breathing new life into it while honoring the traditions of the past. She says many of the children who visit are surprised to find out what school was like back then, including how patriotic and religious kids were in the classroom, starting each day reading Bible scriptures. Some are glad disciplinary measures have changed over the years and say it is unfair that teachers were given the authority to discipline students immediately and with final determination back then.

The children get to experience what class was like at the turn of the century in the beautifully restored Little Red Schoolhouse. According to

Little Red Schoolhouse on Shankland in Willoughby. *Photo by author.*

Weber, much of the structure is original, including the wooden floors and windows, but as with any historic building, repairs are regularly needed, and renovations are ongoing and made possible by much-needed support from the community.

Although from the outside, everything about the Little Red Schoolhouse looks seamlessly original, one pivotal piece was added after the move: the cupola that holds the bell. Today, children love to ring the bell by pulling on a rope hanging inside the front door, but teachers like Miss Dowling used to ring a hand bell to let children know class was beginning or over for the day.

8

PARKS AND RECREATION

PENITENTIARY GLEN

Penitentiary Glen is a popular park year-round, with miles of hiking trails, wetlands, outdoor play areas, wildlife and nature centers, but the focal point of this Lake Metroparks park is the gulley carved right through it.

The winding gully has its own microclimate that remains several degrees cooler, allowing for plants to grow that are normally found north of Ohio. In fact, the plants are so sensitive to temperature that even though the gorge only spans about one hundred feet, different varieties grow on each side because the north side gets more sunshine.

The name Penitentiary Glen has several stories behind it, none of which have been proven to be true. One centers on two men who escaped from prison and decided the gully would be a great hideout. However, they couldn't leave the gully to get supplies, so they lived out their days in a different sort of penitentiary. According to another story, the name came from the depth and the steep sides of the gorge, lined with 320-million-year-old rock layers, making it extremely difficult to climb up from the deepest parts. A legend connected to Kirtland's Mormon history says that in the nineteenth century, a group of Mormons leaving the city due to persecution hid in the gully and decided to live there for a while before heading West, leaving markings on the rock walls, which so far have not been found. Yet one other tale says it was used as a natural prison by Native Americans or even during the Civil War.

For many years, this unique geographical land was a summer resort and working farm owned by Samuel "Sam" Halle and his family. Samuel co-owned the Halle Bros Company with his brother Salmon Halle. This was one of Cleveland's leading department stores at the time, employing up to two thousand people in 1918.

According to Margueritte "Muffi" Sherwin, Sam's great-granddaughter, Sam met his wife, Blanche Murphy, while visiting his store competitor in downtown Cleveland. Sam heard people talking about the lovely saleswomen who worked at the cosmetics counter at Higbees Department Store, and it had become quite a popular gathering place. So, Sam went over to investigate, offered one of the sales ladies a job and later married her. Muffi says her great-grandparents' marriage in 1901 was so controversial—because he was Jewish and she was Catholic—that the *Cleveland Press* sent a spy to make sure it actually happened.

The Halles bought the 184-acre property in 1912 for $12,000. It contained several farm buildings, including a small log cabin said to date to the French and Indian War. It is located near the edge of the gorge on the eastern end of the property. Samuel and Blanche quickly expanded the cabin into a bigger house, using stone brought by horse from the bottom of the gorge, to accommodate their five children, Katherine "Kay," Walter, Margaret, Jane and Ann. Since there was no plumbing, water was pumped by hand from an outdoor well, and the family fondly referred to their outhouse as Sunset Villa.

The Halles used a swinging suspension bridge to cross the gorge to a smaller home known as Ann's Cottage. It was one of the first prefab homes, with parts shipped from the manufacturer in Massachusetts and assembled on the property. It was named after Ann, the youngest daughter, who loved spending time in the house. It was surrounded by fountains, formal English gardens and a silo converted into a sun tower with a spiral staircase.

Because Sam Halle made frequent buying trips to Europe, Maude Doolittle, who became known as Doody, was hired to take care of the children. She was a naturalist and spent days exploring nature with the children; identifying plants, trees and fungi in the woods; and establishing their love of nature. The gorge became their natural playground.

Although the Halles only lived on the property in the summer, the Burnett family managed the farm and lived there year-round from 1917 to 1940, growing corn and raising cattle, pigs and chickens. They lived in a home on the north edge of the estate, where the present visitor parking lot is. They were hard-working and kind-hearted and were known to leave boxes of food on people's back porches during the Depression. John was an innovative man who experimented with new farming techniques and built beautiful stone terraces and patios on the estate, along with the swinging bridge.

The Halle property on Kirtland-Chardon Road (once called Snake Hill) also had apple and peach orchards and a vineyard (where there is said to be a piece of a meteor in the nearby woods), granary, dairy, creamery, tool shed, icehouse and corncrib. There was a small airfield because Sam owned a small plane and loved flying, horse stables (all of the Halles enjoyed riding), tennis courts and a nearby swimming pool and bathhouse. According to Lake Metroparks archives, the large swimming pool was built near the main house in the early 1930s, after the children discovered a black snake while swimming in one of their creek pools. It was built next to the creek with icy cold spring water pumped in through a real lion's head mounted on the stone wall, brought back by Walter, when he went on safari in Africa.

The farm was the site of the Kirtland Pioneer Picnic, held each August. The picnics ran from 1926 to 1941 (discontinued during World War II) and were like a family reunion. Generous prizes were brought in by the Halle Bros truck for contest winners. Ice cream, cold drinks, cracker jacks and candy canes were sold at a refreshment stand. A picnic dinner was enjoyed at noon, and sports contests were held throughout the day, including a ballgame, a lemon throw, nail driving, croquet, a boys' race, an egg contest, archery and a horseshoe tournament. The girls had a needle-and-thread contest, and a watermelon eating race was held for anyone hungry enough to partake.

In the late 1930s, life was about to change on the farm. John Burnett woke in the middle of the night to see the barn was on fire. Even visitors, enjoying the night dancing, at the Kirtland Country Club could see the blaze. Although Mr. Burnett tried to put it out with buckets of water, it burned to the ground. The cause was believed to be spontaneous combustion from the new hay stacked in the barn. The old barn and granary were saved, but this seemed to be the beginning of the end for Halle Farm.

Samuel Halle visited the farm until his death in 1954. The Halle estate was then inherited by all five children and placed under management of Cleveland Trust because they were all living elsewhere. It was rented out to a family who took care of it for fifteen years and then Lake Metroparks bought it in the 1970s. The Halle family gave the Kirtland Fire Department permission to burn down their old cottage in 1970 as a training exercise because it was in disrepair. As soon as the park system bought the property, it began renovating the old stable house, which had housed the caretakers' quarters, five stalls for riding horses and a five-car garage. The modern

Ruins of Halle estate suspension bridge across the ravine at Penitentiary Glen. *Photo by author.*

program center was added to the original building, and the stable house is used once again as the nature center, allowing visitors to learn about and enjoy nature, just as the Halles did so many years ago.

Although nature has reclaimed much of the original Halle site, trail maps for self-guided tours are available in the nature center. Visitors who follow the H trail posts will find there are still remnants of the past in the landscape, including rhododendrons, English ivy, pachysandra and myrtle (vinca), along with stone steps, columns, walls and stone-lined paths. The two stone posts where the suspension bridge used to be are still visible, but the bridge is long gone.

Kay Halle

One of Sam and Blanche's children, Kay Halle, described as a tall, slender, blond beauty, became a well-known socialite but was much more than just a pretty face. Kay was a well-known journalist, radio commentator, author and confidante to many of the most influential leaders of the day.

146

In the early 1930s, she lived in London and wrote a weekly column for the *Cleveland News*. Through this position, she became friends with many artists and dignitaries, including British wartime leader Sir Winston Churchill and his family. She was first acquainted with the Churchills through Winston's son, Randolph, when he stayed at the Halle residence during his 1931 visit to Cleveland. The next year, while in England, Kay stayed at Chartwell, Churchill's country house. Her friendship with Sir Winston lasted until his death in 1965, and she even published two books about him.

After returning to the United States, she wrote for the *Cleveland Press* and the *Plain Dealer*. In 1939, she broadcasted a fifteen-minute radio series called *Know Your City* through Cleveland CBS affiliate WGAR, conducting interviews with Cleveland greats, like baseball legend Bob Feller. Kay also provided intermission commentary for the Cleveland Orchestra.

In the 1940s, Halle served as an executive in the Office of Strategic Services (OSS), which was a U.S. wartime intelligence agency during World War II.

After the war, she moved to Washington, D.C., but continued to do a series for WGAR as its Washington correspondent. She developed personal and professional relationships with many political figures through this role, including Presidents Franklin D. Roosevelt, Harry S. Truman, Dwight D. Eisenhower and John F. Kennedy. In the '60s, Kay worked on Senator John F. Kennedy's presidential campaign, organizing the Cleveland Citizens for Kennedy.

It is said that she influenced President Kennedy's decision to name Sir Winston Churchill as the first Honorary American Citizen in 1963, an honor that Sir Winston was said to consider his most prized public tribute.

Although she never married, she once showed a friend a list of sixty-four men who had proposed to her, including Randolph Churchill (who she had dated, according to her family). She died in 1997 at the age of ninety-three.

The Village of Waite Hill

Pioneers discovered Waite Hill in about 1820. It was thickly wooded and almost inaccessible on the north and west sides, but it was reachable from the south. The view of the river valley, along with rich soil, drew twenty-eight-year-old brothers Alvan and Erastus Waite, who came from Onondaga County, New York, to clear land their father, William Waite, had purchased.

Waite Hill bird sanctuary sign. *Photo by author.*

At the time, Waite Hill was known as Chagrin, formerly the township of Carlton, but it was named Waite Hill after these early pioneers who built some of the first log cabins.

The village of Waite Hill is a unique community that retains its expansive beauty thanks to plans put in place by original large landowners. They created a community layout with regulations on property size to protect their land and investment. One of the reasons Waite Hill, incorporated in 1928, has kept its charm of a bygone era while nearby cities fill with business districts and development is due to the planning and zoning begun by these early owners that are still implemented today. For example, residents in the middle of the village must have a minimum of ten acres, unless grandfathered in. It's also suggested that those preparing to build do so near the tree line rather than in an open field.

Marguerite "Muffi" Sherwin is a great-granddaughter of one of the original large property owners in Waite Hill, John Sherwin Sr., a successful businessman and president of Cleveland Trust Bank, and his wife, Frances McIntosh. She has fond memories of growing up playing with siblings and cousins on her family's estate, South Farm, a one-thousand-acre working farm with sheep and Ayrshire cows.

Waite Hill is also known as a bird sanctuary, and Muffi's grandparents, Francis McIntosh Sherwin (an early mayor of Waite Hill) and Margaret Halle Sherwin (daughter of Samuel Halle, co-owner of Halle Bros Co.), were always interested in birds. Margaret, however, was an ornithologist who banded birds and taught her grandchildren a lot about the different types of birds that flew onto their property. According to Muffi, her grandmother kept meticulous records of the birds visiting Waite Hill, along with their flight patterns. Her records are now kept at the Cleveland Natural History Museum and play an important role in preserving vital information about various bird species and how they've been affected by climate change.

Muffi's late father, Brian Sherwin, was also passionate about nature preservation. He created the Waite Hill Land Conservancy, consisting of 297 acres from the Sherwin's South Farm property, along with property from several other large landowners. In 2012, the conservancy merged with the Western Reserve Land Conservancy, ensuring that Waite Hill will continue to maintain wide open spaces and that the animal and plant species unique to the area, situated in a large watershed of the Chagrin River, are preserved.

The late mayor Arthur D. Baldwin II also played a big role in Waite Hill land preservation. He had an important and lasting impact on the village over his decades of service to the community and was mayor from 1966 to 2012, when he retired after forty-six years, the longest tenure of any mayor in Lake County history and longest continuous service as a mayor in Ohio.

According to his wife of sixty years, Margot Baldwin, not much has changed in Waite Hill since she and her husband moved to the village decades ago. "My husband worked hard to preserve the community with its rural atmosphere and open spaces," she explained.

Under his leadership, many of the original estates have been maintained. Although some historic buildings have been lost to time, residents continue to carefully restore their homes and even build additions to accommodate the needs of their modern families.

Of the many legacies Mayor Baldwin left behind, Mrs. Baldwin believes she knows what he would be most proud of: "He would feel

Arthur Baldwin, long-time mayor of Waite Hill. *Photo courtesy of private collection.*

his important legacy would be maintaining the rural feel while working to break the perception that Waite Hill is only an exclusive community when it's actually diverse and inclusive in many ways."

The Kirtland Country Club

The Kirtland Country Club on Kirtland Road was once the estate of Henry and Josephine Everett. Their stone mansion, now the clubhouse, was built in 1910, and their expansive property was originally known as Leo Doro Farms.

Henry A. Everett was born in Cleveland in 1856. The Everetts were married in 1886 and had two children, Dorothy and Leolyn. Henry was quickly becoming a prominent businessman in the public utility industries, independent telephone companies and electric lighting corporations throughout the Midwest.

In the 1890s, he became president of the Cleveland Electric Railway Company and Ohio's first interurban line, the Akron, Bedford & Cleveland, in a time when Cleveland was emerging as a national leader in electric railways. Whereas city streetcar lines helped passengers maneuver around a downtown, the interurbans were connecting small towns and villages with the city center.

Everett and business partner Edward Moore (who built Mooreland Mansion) formed the Everett-Moore Syndicate in 1901 to operate the Lake Shore Electric Railway Co., a merger of four interurban railways. Together, they also developed Willoughbeach Amusement Park in present-day Willowick as a lucrative stop on their Cleveland, Painesville & Eastern (CP&E) rail line.

Surprisingly, the Everetts might have never actually lived in their beautiful mansion. According to Mark Petzing, general manager and chief operating officer of the Kirtland Country Club, the Everetts bought the property and went to Europe on their honeymoon. While away, they asked their architect to alter their original plans and double the size of the dining room, but when they returned, they discovered the whole house had been doubled in size, and they felt it was too large to live in.

Henry died in 1917, and although Leo Doro Farms might not have been quite what the Everetts wanted, a group of local businessmen and philanthropists saw great potential in the property.

A book in the club's archives, called *Kirtland Country Club*, printed in 1927, reads: "The idea of establishing a country club in the vicinity of Mentor and Willoughby was first seriously discussed in the spring of 1920 and during the summer of that year Mr. David Z. Norton and Mr. Edward W. Moore had several conferences with Mrs. Henry A. Everett in regard to purchasing her beautiful estate of Leo Doro Farms, just east of Willoughby."

In the following weeks, the founding members met with seventy-eight friends who committed to $500,000 in subscriptions to join the proposed club. Since financial backing was secured, the subscribers bought the estate, including 580 acres and twenty-five buildings, from Josephine for $350,000. An organization committee was appointed, including "Messrs, D.Z. Norton [who became the first club president], F.A. Scott, John Sherwin, and A.D. Baldwin, and the name of the Kirtland Country Club [was] selected." Their names are still familiar in the community today, and many of their descendants remain members of the club, including those of the Everetts.

The club officially opened on July 9, 1921, with 233 charter members. In the first year, $828,000 (including the purchase price) was spent on extensive alterations, including adding amenities, such as a golf course (the first course designed in the United States by one of the premier golf course architects of the time Captain C.H. Alison), a locker house, polo fields, an in-ground swimming pool and four tennis courts.

With unique natural elements and varied geographic features of the course came several hurdles for golfers. Before the modern suspension bridge was added, they took a rope-pulled boat across the Chagrin River to get from the twelfth to the thirteenth hole. There's also a very steep ravine with a seventy-to-eighty-foot drop, making it hard to get up from the lower holes. Industrialist, ardent golfer and senior member of the club Harry Colby was forbidden by his doctor from playing this part of the course because of the severe climb from hole seventeen to eighteen. He was, however, determined to play and proposed financing and creating an escalator to carry golfers from the lower holes.

According to a framed letter hanging in the halls of the club, Robert C. Norton, club president at the time, thanked Colby for offering to pay for the cost but said the directors had approved $10,000 from the club. Just a few years after the club opened, in 1925, a cable car was installed, connecting golfers from the lower holes. A modernized version is still used today.

Even in the Kirtland Country Club's early days, it was known as one of the best courses around and attracted top professional golfers, like Bobby Jones, who played in exhibition golf matches at the club. His crowning glory was the grand slam of 1930, when he became the only golfer to win the British Amateur, British Open, U.S. Amateur and U.S. Open in the same year.

For over half a century, members enjoyed social and sporting activities at the club, but on August 3, 1975, disaster struck. The clubhouse went up in flames, and only the massive stone walls were left standing. The cause is unknown, although it might have been electrical or from a lightning strike.

Margot Baldwin, club member and widow of the late Arthur Baldwin (long-time mayor of the village of Waite Hill, past club president and grandson of one of the club's early founders, Arthur D. Baldwin), recalls many happy years spent at the club with her husband and their four daughters. She says she will always remember the day of the fire because it was her second child's birthday. Baldwin says her husband, who was interested in photography at the time, went to the club the day after the blaze to document the ruins. His photos were an important reference when the clubhouse was rebuilt because they showed builders how everything looked before the fire.

Building engineer Mark Morse has worked at the club since the 1970s, following in the footsteps of his father, who worked there before him. He recalls that when the fire broke out, several members saved some of the club valuables, including a large dark wood Tiffany grandfather clock. He said they flipped it on its side and hauled it to safety. It stands, perfectly preserved, in the clubhouse today.

The main section of the clubhouse was destroyed, but 90 percent of the outside stone was saved and reused. It was rebuilt on the old foundation, replicating the original building in size, style and materials. The use of old and new stone is evident on the clubhouse chimney today—one half of the stone appears newer, and the other half is a darker shade.

Other reminders of the past include a stone plaque with Henry Everett's initials, "H.A.E. 1909," on one end of the building and the original garage, next to the clubhouse. Although the wading pond that used to sit on the back lawn of the clubhouse is gone, the stone pillars marking the entrance to a long walkway from its early days remain. Other pillars and pieces of foundation from original structures marked as dwellings and ancillary buildings to the polo fields are on private property and are no longer owned by the club. The club once expanded far past the current property lines and used to stretch under what is now State Route I-90.

The Kirtland Country Club continues to thrive with more than three hundred members who enjoy an expansive property rooted in history and tradition. It was created by some of the great industrialists of the nineteenth

Right: The grandfather clock saved from the fire at Kirtland Country Club. *Photo by author.*

Below: Part of the original building at Kirtland Country Club. *Photo by author.*

and twentieth centuries, who mined coal and iron, forged steel and ran shipping lines and railroads. The reminders are all around, but perhaps the most symbolic, although often unnoticed, is a boulder with traces of iron ore that sits on the golf course's first tee, symbolizing one of the great industrious contributions of its early founders.

WILDWOOD CULTURAL CENTER

No matter the time of year, visitors can be seen meandering along paths, among the trees and attending various programs and events at Wildwood Cultural Center. It is one of Mentor's most beautiful parks and is a sought-after location for family photo sessions. John and May Oliver saw the beauty in the property more than a century ago, when they picked the location for their summer home.

John G. Oliver was a prominent Cleveland industrialist in the early 1900s, known for drafting the plans for the largest telescope of its time while working at Warner and Swazey Inc. in Cleveland. According to his granddaughter May Targett, his portion of the design involved the controls for directing the telescope.

He was later a founder of Bardons & Oliver, a machine tool firm that still exists today. While developing the business, the Olivers visited England, staying with John's English business partner, whose home was in a, then trendy, Victorian-era Tudor-style country house.

As John's business flourished, the Olivers followed in the steps of other wealthy Clevelanders and decided to build a summer home in Lake County. Named Wildwood Estate, it stood on thirty-four acres of land on Little Mountain Road in Mentor. Architect Abram Garfield, son of President James Garfield, was commissioned to build the home, and construction lasted nearly three years. During this time, the Olivers and their children, Margaret, Hortense and Lockwood, traveled from their home in Cleveland's University Circle to spend time at their developing summer estate, living in the estate's barn during the summers of 1906 and 1907.

In 1908, when construction was completed, Wildwood Estate, inspired by their trip to England, became one of the earliest examples of the English Tudor revival style in northeast Ohio. It contains twenty-five rooms, including nine bedrooms and eight fireplaces, and was run by a staff of six.

Wildwood Manor House. *Photo by Korene Engelking.*

According to May Targett, after serious illness of her mother, Margaret, in 1915, when May was just ten years old, John built her a playhouse in the woods behind their home. (Her brothers were eleven and nine years older, so she had the playhouse to herself.) It was a small brick house with electricity, running water and a miniature kitchen with working stove.

The Wildwood Estate was also a working farm with vegetable and flower gardens, apple orchards and cows on the property. The milk, processed in nearby Kirtland, was transported to the Olivers' Cleveland home when they didn't need it at Wildwood.

The family continued to enjoy their time at Wildwood for years. In 1939, shortly after John Oliver's death, his daughter, Margaret Oliver Collacott, and her husband, Robert Collacott, inherited the estate. According to May Targett, it was around this time that Wildwood got a freezer for storing food, which was one of the first of its kind in Lake County. The Collacotts decided to have the home winterized for year-round use and began living there permanently by 1949.

May Targett has many fond memories of growing up on the estate, and she and her sister, Catherine DeWitt, inherited Wildwood in 1973, when their mother died. Their father continued living in the home until his death three years later, and the sisters continued to visit and maintain the property for several more years.

"By 1980, we realized that our use scarcely justified ownership of the property and were thrilled by Mentor city's offer to buy it," May recalled. City of Mentor officials saw the potential of preserving the property as a park, and a year after the purchase, it was placed on the National Register of Historic Places, which made it eligible for federal grants, and the city began restoring the historic estate.

Wildwood Manor House is now the heart of the Wildwood Cultural Center and is one of Lake County's finest jewels, a park for all to enjoy while preserving its beautiful historic architecture and natural surroundings.

May Targett says she is happy to see others enjoying the property she used to call home, "I am delighted that Mentor found a use for the house, which seems to bring happy experiences to so many. And I know that both Mother and her mother would be delighted also."

Rabbit Run Theater

In north Madison, close to Lake Erie, there is a barn that has been a mainstay in the community for generations. When it was built in the 1920s, it sat on the Klump farm, known at the time for growing broccoli as its main crop. That broccoli attracted rabbits from all around, which led to the name people know today, Rabbit Run Theater.

In 1918, the Klump family bought the working farm, with goats, horses and rabbits, from the Stevens family. Then in 1940, Will Klump Jr. and his sister, Rooney Klump, who loved theater, became involved with a small group of thespians called the Penny Players, performing in a barn owned by Donald and Jean Scheier located on Hubbard Road in Madison-on-the-Lake, across the street from the Madison Dairy Queen. Will, who became enamored of acting in college, performed in two productions that summer.

However, the start of World War II quickly put an end to the Penny Players, as Will headed off to war. In 1946, when the war was over and Will returned, there seemed to be more need than ever to entertain and brighten people's spirits. In a matter of just three weeks, the Klump family converted the old horse barn into a theater capable of seating almost two hundred people.

The theater opened its doors for the first time on July 3, 1946, with a production of *Here Today*. The troupe was made of nine actors, all of whom were World War II veterans, and actresses, and they produced nine plays

Rabbit Run Theater, 1947. *Courtesy of Bill Birk.*

that first year, with the theater consistently filled to capacity by the middle of the season. According to Bill Birk, who has been the historian of Rabbit Run Theater since 1988, the theater started out with comedies and a few dramas. They didn't perform the first musical at Rabbit Run until 1954, but lately, musicals are the more popular plays.

After several years, college students were recruited to perform from Ohio, New York and Pennsylvania, and Will and Rooney's mother, Marney Klump, graciously housed many of them in her own home for nearly two decades.

Birk, who is writing a book about the theater, says barn theaters were quite common at the time, since there was no air conditioning in the big theater districts, like Broadway. So, in the summer months, many of the actors traveled to open-air barn theaters to perform. Now only a few remain in each state.

Many famous actors performed at Rabbit Run Theater before they were well known, including Dustin Hoffman; Charles Grodin; Sandy Dennis (who won an Academy Award for her role in *Who's Afraid of Virginia Wolf*); Jim Backus (who played the millionaire on *Gilligan's Island*) and his wife, Henny; Jessica Tandy; and Marge Redmond (known for her role in *The Flying Nun*).

In 1953, Jim and Henny Backus were visiting family in Cleveland when they ended up starring in a production of *The Man Who Came to Dinner* at Rabbit Run. It wasn't originally on the theater's roster, but since Jim had recently broken his leg during a fall at his home, the theater accommodated him with the role of a leading man who was, appropriately, supposed to have a broken leg.

Just a few years later, in 1955, theater attendance was going strong and a $25,000 stage house was added, increasing theater seating to about three hundred. It became an Actor's Equity Association (AEA) theater in 1955, and during the 1956 season, it fell on hard times due to the high cost of an Equity stage and union wages. It was also competing with other local theaters that had greater resources and could attract bigger names, combined with a decline in visitors to Madison's once-thriving summer resort area. It closed its doors in 1957, and the Klumps would no longer manage the theater. Several production companies leased the theater in the 1960s, and the final production was in the middle of the 1967 season, when money ran out.

In 1979, a group called Friends of Rabbit Run Theater came together and raised $1,000 to lease the theater, marking a new beginning. The theater opened in 1980, with *Joseph and the Amazing Technicolor Dreamcoat* and has remained open since. Each year, around eight thousand theatergoers attend the summer productions. In 2000, Friends of Rabbit Run Theater merged with Western Reserve Fine Arts Association to create Rabbit Run Community Arts Association, which offers year-round programming and curriculum in the arts.

Rabbit Run Theater was, and still is, a training ground for various roles in the theater, not only for the many actors who have gone on to make a name for themselves in TV and film but also the behind-the-scenes producers and technicians who learned their craft at Rabbit Run.

Don Balluck, who had been an actor at the theater, went on to write many of the episodes of the *Little House on the Prairie* series. He also wrote for a number of well-known TV series, including *Hawaii Five-O*, *Starsky and Hutch* and *Fantasy Island*.

Chris Langhart started doing technical work at the theater when he was only fourteen years old. He spent eight years there working on the lighting and sound for various productions. He went on to become a professor at New York University, worked at the legendary concert venue in New York City Filmore East and served as site director and designer of the famed Woodstock music festival in 1969. At Woodstock, he managed the backstage area, medical tent, free kitchen and VIP area. He also built a bridge connecting artists with the backstage area, which was across the road behind the massive stage, and the stage itself.

In *Woodstock: Back to Yasgur's Farm*, Langhart said, "Backstage, I designed a tent for the performers, and the construction was headed by Richard Hartman. The live sound mixing was done out in the audience, but one had to climb onto the stage to see which microphones were working. We had no quick access to the stage for sound persons." Perhaps his ability to quickly improvise began in his earliest days in lighting and sound at Rabbit Run Theater.

Birk says there are many up-and-coming actors and technicians at the theater today, and he can see many of them going on to work in the industry as professionals. He says that some people might know Rabbit Run Theater is at the site of an old barn in Madison, but he wants them to understand it's so much more than that.

"I want them to realize this is a training ground for professional entertainment in all different capacities. So many people have gone on to do great things in their expertise, whether lighting, sound, set design or the acting or singing part of it," Bill explains. "This is the kind of place that people can get that experience and get the help to live their dream to perform and provide excellent entertainment."

9

Nearly Lost and Threatened

Mentor Marsh

Mentor Marsh was once the old channel of the Grand River, emptying into Lake Erie five miles west of its present outlet. In the spring of 1797, returning surveyor Charles Parker established the first settlement in Mentor Marsh when he chose the spot to build his cabin. Before 1810, farms in the township were five dollars an acre, which helped settlements expand rapidly.

A settler, ten-year-old Clarissa Munson (Bronson), wrote there was a "miasma arising from [the] stagnant pool [of the] marsh," extending from Black Brook to where it empties into the lake. She said so many early settlers became sick that they abandoned their newly cleared land and homes to find a healthier spot to live farther south along the Ridge Road, known today as Mentor Avenue.

The marsh is a haven for plant and animal life but was almost destroyed to make way for industry more than one hundred years ago.

In 1901, just before selling his Carnegie Company to U.S. Steel, Andrew Carnegie, self-made steel tycoon, was planning to create a massive steel and shipping complex in Conneaut. Area competitors who were concerned he would overtake the steel and coal market began secretly buying over two thousand acres of land in the Mentor Marsh. At the same time, they were making deals with the railroads to create lines in the area because they thought Mentor was the perfect location. It was near Cleveland, already had three railroad lines and was right on Lake Erie. Local papers began

Mentor Marsh conservancy sign, 1964. *Courtesy of Special Collections, Cleveland State University Library.*

discussing the possibility of using the marsh as a steel complex, but the entire project was stopped before it even began by one man—Peter Hitchcock.

Hitchcock, who came from a wealthy Cleveland family, refused to sell his land at the west end of the marsh, adjacent to where Black Creek flowed into Lake Erie. For several years, he turned down offers from U.S. Steel, which had joined forces with local investors because they decided Carnegie's project in Conneaut would be too far from Cleveland. However, investors eventually turned their attention away from Mentor and toward Lorain on Cleveland's west side, where a facility was built.

In the 1960s, the marsh was threatened again when salt mine tailings were dumped into Blackbrook Creek, and by the '70s, most of the marsh plants and swamp forest trees had died, and it was being overtaken by nonnative reed grass.

During an effort to rescue the blighted site in the 1960s, the Cleveland Museum of Natural History accepted custodianship of the marsh to preserve the land and wildlife. Money was raised to buy an 80-acre tract of land owned by the New York Central Railroad, nearby Morton Salt Company donated 320 acres and Diamond Alkali donated 90 acres for marsh preservation. Thanks to additional gifts and purchases, the Mentor Marsh Preserve now consists of 691 acres of land.

The marsh remained undeveloped and was designated as a National Natural Landmark by the National Park Service in 1966 because it's one of the most species-rich sites on the Great Lakes shoreline, an important breeding ground for fish, and a National Audubon Society Important Birding Area. It also became Ohio's first state nature preserve through the Ohio Department of Natural Resources and is one of the largest natural marshes on the Lake Erie shoreline.

In 2004, the Cleveland Museum of Natural History began a large-scale restoration of Mentor Marsh, and since then, dozens of native plant species and rare birds have returned. In recent years, more than nineteen thousand plants, with twenty-three species native to the marsh, have been planted at the site.

SOUTH LEROY MEETING HOUSE

The South LeRoy Meeting House at 13668 Painesville Warren Road is the oldest historical landmark in Leroy Township. It's currently home to the LeRoy Heritage Association (LHA), a group dedicated to preserving the township's history and heritage, and the Leroy history museum. According to Lori Watson, treasurer and historian of the association, the building was originally constructed as a modest country church and was built by early Leroy Township pioneer Henry Brakeman.

Brakeman's sons and neighbors helped him construct it by gathering lumber from the land within a quarter mile of the building, sawing it and planing it by hand. The sturdy timber frame was assembled and enclosed in 1822, but Brakeman continued to work evenings by tallow candlelight for the next decade to complete the church. It was said to have been put together with prayer and handmade nails.

The church held Sunday services and hosted social events and school graduations. In 1851, Brakeman deeded the South LeRoy Meeting House to the Methodist Episcopal Church, and it later became known as the Brakeman Church.

In August 1936, many of the men in the community spent two days reroofing the church while their wives prepared and served dinner at the Grange each night. A month later, more residents donated their time to wire the church with electric lights.

More than thirty years later, in 1964, the Brakeman Church had outgrown the building and moved to the newly constructed Leroy Community Chapel. The original Brakeman Church building sat abandoned and decaying, until it was condemned by the fire department in 1972.

A few years later, a group of township residents decided to save the landmark and formed the LeRoy Heritage Association in 1975, using the historic spelling for Leroy by capitalizing the *R*. They worked to restore the church to its original state, based on their research, with the help of donations of time, money, labor and materials.

They fixed and painted the windows and siding, the interior lathe and horsehair plaster walls and wide plank floors. Many who had attended Brakeman Church took the pews and pulpit when it closed to use as decor in their homes, and some stored them in their barns because they had expected the church to eventually be torn down. When the restoration began in the '70s, community members brought back the pews and even paid to have them restored. In fact, each pew has a brass name plate on it of the person who sponsored to have it repaired, reinstalled and painted.

In 1976, when the Methodist Episcopal Church officially turned over ownership of the building to Leroy Township, with the condition that it must be preserved for historic reasons, the LeRoy Heritage Association arranged to lease the building from the township for one dollar a year. Then in 1979, it was placed on the National Register of Historic Places.

South Leroy Meeting House (Brakeman Church) in 1930. *Courtesy of LeRoy Heritage Association.*

Even though the building was restored, it has begun to deteriorate over the last few decades, so the LeRoy Heritage Association began restoring the building again in 2014. The group has completed exterior work and has repaired and painted the plaster walls on the interior, but it is continuing to restore the inside and is creating displays of historical photos, documents and artifacts to showcase the building's history to all who visit.

Watson says the South LeRoy Meeting House is an important piece of history not only to the community but also to her personally, since her family has been in Leroy since 1817 and had ties to the church. "I am really happy that we have been able to restore it so beautifully," she said.

With the community, the LeRoy Heritage Association has saved the church from demolition and turned it into a treasured Leroy landmark.

MADISON SEMINARY

The Madison Seminary, considered by many to be the most haunted building in northeast Ohio, is a sprawling brick building on Middle Ridge Road in Madison Township that is filled with nearly 175 years of history. It was built in 1847 as a private seminary to give the men and women of Lake County a high school and college education.

A large brick building was added to the original wooden structure in 1859, and it remained a school until it closed in 1891, largely due to the decreasing need for private schools, since there was an increase in public education. Although the building was at risk of being demolished because it didn't meet many safety codes, the Ohio Women's Relief Corps saw its potential and determined that it would be a great housing site for Civil War nurses and soldiers' mothers, wives and sisters. The people of Madison and Geneva donated the building, ten acres of land and $1,000 to the cause. It was known as the Madison House or National Relief Corps Home, and in 1891, the still-standing Ohio Cottage was built next to it. Between the two buildings, there were over eighty rooms and thirty-one thousand square feet.

Elizabeth Brown Stiles lived at the National Relief Corps Home near the end of her life and was likely its most well-known resident. She was born in Ashtabula in 1816 and worked as a teacher and seamstress in Chicago for nearly a decade before meeting and marrying Jacob Stiles. She continued to teach when they moved to Kansas in the 1850s and became known for her pro-Union views in the politically divided state.

Madison Seminary, then known as the Madison Home. *Courtesy of Special Collections, Cleveland State University Library.*

One night, her husband, Jacob, was killed at their home by a group of pro-Confederate guerrillas that included young Jesse and Frank James. Soon after, President Abraham Lincoln recruited Elizabeth to serve as a spy and dispatcher for the Union during the Civil War. She disguised herself in a variety of ways, including as a Southern grandmother looking for her granddaughter's wounded father. (The "granddaughter" was actually her thirteen-year-old daughter, Clara.)

Elizabeth was once suspected of being a spy in Missouri and was arrested. By the time her interrogation was over, she had convinced the Confederate officer that she was actually a Rebel spy. Before releasing her, the officer gave her a horse and a better gun.

She continued to work as a spy until 1864, when her identity became known. For the next thirty years, her son cared for her, and she became a resident at the National Relief Corps Home in 1895. She died three years later, at eighty-two, and was buried in the cemetery to the east of the home.

In 1904, the Women's Relief Corps could no longer afford to operate the building and donated it to the State of Ohio. It sat vacant for years and was once again at risk of demolition. In the 1960s, it was taken over by the Ohio Department of Mental Hygiene and Corrections and was renamed Opportunity Village. Select honor inmates from the women's reformatory of Marysville lived and worked in the house. The building also housed disabled women from the Apple Creek State Hospital and was later connected with the Ohio Bureau of Vocational Rehab.

In 1964, it became an extension of the Cleveland State Hospital and Opportunity Village, which officially closed more than a decade later. It served several other purposes over the years, including housing the Madison police in the 1980s. Around that time, it's believed that the building's decor and furniture were burned in a bonfire behind the building. By the 1990s, the police were no longer using the site, and a newspaper ad read, "For rent, historic building, can be leased cheap. Caution: building may be haunted."

In 2016, the building was purchased again, and the owner is working to restore it, preserve its history and share its stories, including many of the haunted variety, by offering public and private tours.

DOWNTOWN WILLOUGHBY FIRE

Downtown Willoughby perfectly captures small-town Americana. In warm-weather months, visitors walk along its tree-lined sidewalks, past hanging flowers and historic brick building storefronts filled with coffee shops, offices, unique retail and restaurants. During the holidays, it's transformed into a lighted winter wonderland, complete with twinkling lights and garland stretching across the street, an enormous Christmas tree, a lighted gazebo and kids lining up to visit with Santa and Mrs. Claus.

The downtown even holds a festival each year called Last Stop Willoughby. It's based on the CP&E interurban trains that had ticket officers and repair/powerhouse buildings in Downtown Willoughby (now housing businesses like Willoughby Brewing Company and Sol), along with the *Twilight Zone* episode believed to be named after it, "Next Stop Willoughby." It's about a man on a train who dreams he is stopping in the quaint town of Willoughby.

Downtown has been an important epicenter for Willoughby and Western Lake County for years and is filled with memories for residents, like Ted Prindle, who grew up in Willoughby and remembers "lighting up the Cleveland Trust Bank at night."

He and his classmates made some lamps in their welding shop class at Willoughby Union High School in 1956, which the bank agreed to display in the front window. Prindle remembers making a capacity-operated relay out of used parts, with a big aluminum hand placed on the outside bank window, allowing people to touch the lamps and light them up inside.

Downtown Willoughby at Christmas, looking south on Erie Street. *Courtesy of Willoughby Historical Society.*

About seventy-five years earlier, downtown Willoughby was ablaze for an entirely different reason—it was on fire. It suffered several fires over the years, but the biggest, according to the Willoughby Historical Society, struck in 1883 and 1885.

In 1883, a fire consumed all of the buildings on the west side of Erie Street, from the Bond Building (the three-story building that still exists today) south to the corner of West Spaulding and west on Spaulding to Clark Avenue (called First Street then). Two years later, a second fire blazed through buildings on the east side of Erie Street from today's Austin Building (which houses the restaurant Ballantine) south to East Spaulding.

The first fire, described in an issue of the Willoughby paper, the *Independent*, on November 9, 1883, was the most destructive fire that ever occurred in Willoughby. Stores, dwellings, barns, horses and mules were all consumed. The article reads, "From the best information we can obtain, the fire commenced in the south-east corner of Mr. T.S. Harbach's large barn in rear of the store on the west side of Erie street."

Night watchman Morgan said that while eating lunch at his headquarters in Barnes Bros., he saw a light but thought it was a lantern. "On going out he discovered flames bursting from the corner of the barn, the wind blowing from the north-west a perfect gale. He at once gave the alarm, and ran to the barn, but could gain no entrance. In a few minutes the barn was all in flames and fell with a loud crash."

The buildings nearby were made of wood and "burned like tinder." The last building contained oil and gasoline, but most of it was rolled out safely away from the fire. The fire had reached the corner of Spaulding and Erie Streets, and the brick hardware store of Kennedy & Son soon fell. As the fire continued to spread, the article says the "towering block of Mr. Bond stood like a rock, thereby saving the progress of the flames, and but for this there would have been no *Independent* office, and the spot where we now write marked only by a blackened waste."

It says it was "almost by superhuman exertion that the dwellings on the south side of Spaulding and the stores on the east side of Erie were saved." Their destruction had seemed inevitable until men, women and children, since there was no city fire department, "worked like heroes," dumping water to put out the fire.

Homes and shops—a grocery store, barbershop, boot and shoe shop, marble shop, furniture shop, drugstore and jeweler, among others—suffered thousands of dollars in damages. Although the community came together to help extinguish the blaze, there were reports after the fire of stealing from the damaged buildings.

Also, amazingly, there was no loss of life, "but lame backs, peeled shins, singed hair, and blistered hands are quite common."

The fire was suspected to have started in a barn, but a definite source wasn't determined. After the fire, many property owners decided to rebuild using brick instead of wood, much of which is what we see today.

VENICE OF LAKE ERIE

The lure of the lake draws members to the Mentor Harbor Yacht Club (MHYC) to enjoy the panoramic view from inside the historic Spanish-style building, outside on the patio or lawn or on a yacht on the ever-changing water.

It's been nearly a century since the club was officially formed on Coronada Drive in Mentor, but for hundreds of years, the site was a marsh forming an uneven break in the otherwise clearly etched shoreline of Lake Erie. The marsh, full of fish, game and wild fowl, was a popular summer camping ground for Native Americans. According to the book *Mentor Harbor Yachting Club*, not many years ago, you could see the charred rocks in the fire holes of Indian encampments, and a large Indian burial ground was visible on the wooded slopes just east of the harbor.

In the 1800s, a log road made of closely laid heavy square timbers was constructed across the marsh for prospectors of bog iron, and it became the most traveled route from the Headlands westward.

Toward the end of the nineteenth century, a channel had broken through, and with relatively high lake levels, some started to realize the potential of creating a harbor at the site of the marsh. A fleet of small lapstrake-hulled fishing sloops was built up, sailing out of the marsh to tend their nets. They docked in open water east of the marsh, and fishermen dried their nets over the reeds and cattails in the marsh's center.

The operation was abandoned in the early 1900s, when the lake level dropped, and the channel was too shallow to use. Although no longer a harbor, the marsh was still a hunting, trapping and fishing paradise. There was a gun club on-site, along with covered boathouses for skiffs and a number of small private cabins.

At the time, the marsh was said to be the wildest area on the shore east of Cleveland. Large bass and pickerel (up to three feet long) were caught in the

Mentor Harbor Yacht Club exterior, 1938. *Courtesy of Special Collections, Cleveland State University Library.*

waterways, along with the largest carp in Lake Erie (some almost as large as a person). There were even reports of massive water and black snakes being found, up to eleven feet long.

At the turn of the century, the marsh almost became the site of a shipping harbor for the booming railroad industry, since the Great Lakes were being used to transport grain down from the Northwest. Men in the railroad industry saw the potential in the harbor to hold a fleet of railroad-owned lake vessels that would have easy access to the inland railroads. A detailed plan was developed by the Baltimore & Ohio Railroad (B&O) to clear out the marsh, construct a harbor and dredge the channel for five miles down the old Grand River to Richmond, with the New York Central constructing the eastern end of the channel. Since the average depth of the marsh was twenty-two feet of soft muck, it could have worked physically. However, even though the railroads were already buying land, their plan quickly came to a halt as the Supreme Court reached a decision in the Granger Rate Cases. The railroads would be able to carry grain from Minnesota as cheaply as the new steamships, which made the idea of a new railroad-run harbor much less appealing. Even though the B&O railroad had already invested in land, it immediately called its plans to a halt.

It wasn't until 1926, two years after Mentor-on-the-Lake was created after separating from Mentor Township, that the development of the harbor really began. While much of the nation was in a financial boom, a small group of businessmen with a vision came up with the idea of a Venice-like real estate development to be built at the marsh. The group was led by Samuel Livingston Mather, son of Samuel Mather, cofounder of Pickands Mather and Company. The younger Mather worked for Cleveland Cliffs Iron Co. and lived in Mentor. He and the rest of the men who created Mentor Harbor Company envisioned the harbor lined with beautiful yachts and a community of fine homes for people who love yachting.

Initial plans included dredging the marsh, building a concrete-walled harbor lined with small boat marinas, constructing a breakwater and a channel and building a Spanish-style clubhouse. They would build one beautiful home and advertise the development to attract buyers to build in the new community that they hoped would become an "American Venice," as advertisements promoted. Brochures stated, "A typical Mentor Harbor

Unfinished "Bridge to Nowhere" on Mentor Lagoons, 1935. *Courtesy of Special Collections, Cleveland State University Library.*

House with a garage for your boat as well as your automobile," and "You are to be congratulated if selected to be a resident of Mentor Harbor."

The Mentor Harbor Company invested over $1 million to dredge the original mouth of the Grand River west of the Mentor Marsh and build the concrete-walled harbor, breakwater and channel. The initial stage of the project was completed in 1929, including the construction of the clubhouse and road system allowing future owners access to their lakefront homes. For many decades, an incomplete bridge to the island (known as the Bridge to Nowhere) to connect residents to the new community was a reminder of the stock market crash that brought their plans to an end. (It was demolished in 2019.)

Even though the community never developed, MHYC did and was incorporated on July 9, 1928. It has grown almost continuously since then. The old Mentor Harbor Company became insolvent by May 1934. Through the following years, S.L. Mather (the club's first commodore) allowed members to use the clubhouse without charge, and by 1935, there were two hundred members and a fleet of ninety boats.

In 1936, the organization was reincorporated as the Mentor Harbor Yachting Club, then boasting 140 boats, power and sail. Over the decades, the clubhouse and MHYC have seen many renovations to keep it moving into the future while retaining its history and charm of the past.

MOORELAND MANSION

Mooreland Mansion on Lakeland Community College's (LCC) campus was once the elegant summer home of Edward William Moore. He was a wealthy Cleveland industrialist who made his fortune in banking, electric railroads and telephone distribution in the late 1800s, alongside business partner Henry Everett.

Together they developed the CP&E Interurban Railway, among many other interurban lines in Ohio and several surrounding states. He even created his own stop at the entrance to his property on Mentor Avenue. Ornamental brick columns stood where Barnes & Noble bookstore is today, at the entrance of Moore's mile-long drive that meandered past farm buildings, through a tunnel of trees and into the forest, where a second set of columns marked the entrance to Moore's grand mansion.

According to LCC historical archives, Moore was born in Canal Dover, Ohio, in 1864 and was the son of German immigrants. (Their original

Mooreland Mansion on Lakeland Community College campus. *Photo by author.*

family name was Mohr.) When he was sixteen years old, he left school and headed to Cleveland, where he got his first job at a banking firm, Everett, Weddell and Co. Then in 1891, Moore and Everett formed the Everett-Moore Syndicate, the first major electric trolley system in the country with trains running to towns east and west of Cleveland. (The interurban trolleys were a popular form of transportation from about 1895 to 1925, falling out of favor among travelers as the automobile became more popular.) The electric trolley systems were less expensive to build than steam railroads and allowed riders to travel quickly between cities. That same year, at twenty-seven years old, Moore married Louise Chamberlain, who was described as a petite woman with big brown eyes and knee-length golden hair.

In 1897, Moore and Everett bought the Eber Norton farm on the west side of Garfield Road and planned to build their summer estates on the property's south ridge. They commissioned Cleveland architect Arthur N. Oviatt to design both homes. (The Kirtland Country Club now stands on the original site of Everett's mansion.)

The twelve-thousand-square-foot Mooreland mansion, completed in 1900, was painted yellow with gold trim and had seven bedrooms and just one

Edward Moore smoking a cigar. *Courtesy of Mooreland Restoration Garden Club/Lakeland Community College.*

bathroom. The property spanned more than one thousand acres of land across Mentor, Willoughby and Kirtland, including the present LCC campus and Great Lakes Mall.

By 1901, Moore had risen to the top in business, despite some financial ups and downs, and was believed to hold more banking stock than anyone else in Cleveland. He worked hard in the industrious city but found respite from the heat in the summer months at Mooreland with his wife and five children, Margaret, Franklyn, Kathryn, Edward Jr. and Elizabeth.

Edward Moore's property originally had four working farms, including North Farm (near the property entrance where Great Lakes Mall now sits), Hill Farm, River Farm and South Farm. These farms were privately leased and managed, providing the Moore family with everything they needed for their stay in the summer months. The farms included many different buildings, like a greenhouse, a hennery, a piggery, a playhouse for the Moore children, several barns, homes for some of the main staff and a two-story, nine-bay garage.

The farms were known to partake in some friendly competition, like raising the largest bull and building the biggest and loveliest barn. In fact,

Mrs. Moore with her children. *Courtesy of Mooreland Restoration Garden Club Lakeland Community College.*

these competitions are believed to have inspired the early days of the Lake County fair.

Around 1907, the Moores hired Cleveland architect J. Milton Dyer (who later designed Cleveland City Hall) to expand their home to a forty-three-room mansion, nearly doubling its size. It included servants' bedrooms on a third level, which strangely had a nine-foot bathtub and expansive porches. When Moore ran an electric line from his railroad stop to his home, it became the first home in Lake County to have electricity.

Landscape architect A. Donald Gray designed expansive landscaping to match the grandeur of Moore's home, including what is believed to be the first in-ground pool in the county, with water pumped up from the Chagrin River; a pergola; beautiful fountains; a formal garden; a rose garden; and a golf course. There was also a deer petting zoo, which was unique at the time because white-tailed deer were eliminated from the state from 1904 to the 1920s, due to land loss from early settlers and over hunting.

Louise Moore loved to garden, even though Mooreland had a full garden staff, and enjoyed having fresh flowers throughout the house. One gardener was assigned the job to create seventy-five flower arrangements a day to decorate the inside of Mooreland. The Moores entertained friends and family outside, using their pool-side pergola as a dancehall and sometimes even as a diving board. They even hosted several famous guests at their home, including the Polish prime minister and renowned pianist Ignacy Paderewski (the grand piano that he played still sits in the home) and First Lady Eleanor Roosevelt.

When Edward Moore became ill in 1926, his son Franklin took over the business that was already in decline, and the final interurban train ran on May 20, 1926. Two years later, Edward passed away just before his sixty-fourth birthday. Since the Moore children were grown and living elsewhere, the family decided to sell their town house on Euclid Avenue in Cleveland, and Louise moved to Mooreland permanently. She lived on the property for nearly three more decades, enjoying the beautiful scenery and tending to her beloved rose gardens, said to have contained well over seven hundred roses. She died when she was ninety years old, after suffering a stroke.

The Moores' daughter Margaret moved back into Mooreland in 1931, after a divorce, and lived there until she died in 1982. Mooreland then became property of the college, according to the original purchase agreement. In the 1960s, the property was split into various parcels, and nearly four hundred acres were sold to the LCC Board of Trustees to develop a new college campus. Mooreland then sat vacant for several years.

It was in such disrepair that the college board originally wanted to demolish it, but Diane Doty, wife of the newly appointed college president Dr. Ralph R. Doty, along with several community members, explored the dilapidated home and found it to be structurally sound, though in need of an enormous restoration.

After experts declared it salvageable, LCC executives, Lake Metroparks, Leadership Lake County and hard-working community members began a decade-long project to restore Mooreland, costing millions of dollars, including hundreds of thousands donated by the community.

Lori Roy is the secretary of the Mooreland Restoration Garden Club and has been committed to preserving the history of Mooreland for several decades. She says she and other members of the club, started in 1989, were able to restore the overgrown gardens by using historic photos and records. Although the garden was in terrible shape, they discovered remnants of what the garden used to look like after removing overgrowth. They were able to use cuttings from original plants, and even some of the Moores' peonies and lilies grew back. They maintain the beautiful gardens to this day, keeping their charm from their earliest days.

Other remnants linger throughout the house, like the wooden partner desk used by both Everett and Moore. A piece of furniture from Moore's private interurban trolley, named Josephine, remains, along with a heavy built-in safe to store jewelry in Louise's bedroom. Two other safes were once in the house—in the kitchen for silverware and in a guest room—but no longer exist.

One of the most interesting features of the house might be a latched window on the top floor, which is different from all of the others and leads out to the roof, where Moore used to climb to a smoking room, since his wife didn't allow him to smoke cigars in the house.

Today Mooreland, listed on the National Register of Historic Places in 1993, is one of the great historic treasures of Lake County. It is rented out for special luncheons, business meetings and weddings.

10

LEGENDS, MYTHS AND DISCOVERIES

GEORGE WASHINGTON ELM

Buttermilk Falls cascades into a ravine in Cleveland Metroparks' North Chagrin Reservation in Willoughby Hills. A wooden lookout bridge along the bike path allows visitors to peak over the edge at the small stream, gurgling over flat cascading rocks. Just a few steps away sits an easily missed small boulder with a weathered plaque on it, facing the falls instead of the nearby bike path. It reads: "George Washington Planting: Trees Given by Western Reserve Chapter D.A.R. 1732–1932."

According to Judy MacKeigan, historian with Cleveland Metroparks, it means that some of the trees in this wooded area might be connected to our country's earliest days. In 1932, Daughters of the American Revolution (DAR) chapters around the country were planting shoots of an elm tree that was purported to be a descendant of the legendary Washington Elm in Cambridge, Massachusetts.

The Washington Elm was the first of a line of six large elm trees that stood in the middle of Garden Street in Cambridge, Massachusetts, and was believed to stand in the same spot where George Washington took command of the Continental army on July 3, 1775. There is no official documentation of this, so although many people visited the tree over the years, the story behind it might have been pure legend.

However, the tree was an important symbol of patriotism and our country's history for many people, so it was carefully cared for over the years,

George Washington Elm plaque at North Chagrin Reservation, Buttermilk Falls in Willoughby. *Photo by author.*

Plaque reads: "George Washington Planting. Trees given by Western Reserve Chapter of D.A.R. (Daughters of the American Revolution) 1932." *Photo by author.*

although some attempts were far from fruitful. At one point, Cambridge city authorities not only cut off dead branches but also smeared tar over the trees "wounds," filled the hollows with cement and braced the remaining limbs with iron bands and rods.

Then, on October 26, 1923, the entire rotting elm was accidentally knocked down while city workers tried to remove yet another dead branch. At the time, experts from a local institution counted 202 rings in its trunk, with the belief that it had probably stopped growing for several years, making the tree about 210 years old.

The tree was sawed into pieces. A large piece of the main trunk was sent to the governor of each state, and a section that showed the rings was polished and presented to the museum at Mount Vernon. Gavels were made out of some of the smaller branches and sent to legislative bodies of each state. Bits and pieces of the tree limbs were cut into fragments, and shoots were then sent around the country to be planted in remembrance of the great Washington Elm.

An article in the *Cleveland Plain Dealer* on July 3, 1932, announces a dedicatory service of a Washington Elm to be planted on the grounds of the Geauga County Court House in Chardon, similar to the planting and plaque found at Buttermilk Falls.

The popular legend of the Washington Elm in Cambridge became a part of American culture as early as the 1830s. Although there are many trees near the plaque at the Metroparks, there is no way to tell which tree or trees might have descended from the famous elm.

LOST NATION ROAD

Lost Nation Road is believed to have been unofficially named in the early 1800s, but how it got its name is a mystery.

One story asserts that a battle between Native Americans and settlers was fought on the site of the old Willoughby Junior High School, where Euclid Avenue and River Street meet. The settlers chased the Indians down a trail north toward the Chagrin River, and once they reached the mouth of the Chagrin, the Native Americans vanished forever, and it became the Lost Nation Trail.

Another legend tells quite a different tale: a group of early settlers with farms along present-day Lost Nation Road became known for their crude behavior and great love of whiskey. The people living in today's downtown Willoughby were mainly Christians who didn't approve of their drinking and grew tired of their boisterous ways, so they began referring to the group in northern Willoughby as the Lost Nation. According to Alan Hitchcox, historian and vice-president of the Willoughby Historical Society, references to Lost Nation in old publications often showed the street name written in quotes as if it wasn't its official name.

Gulls Confectionary and Saloon at the corner of Lost Nation Road and Lakeshore Boulevard, 1945. Presently Marino's Hair Design. *Courtesy of Special Collections, Cleveland State University Library.*

Yet another story tells of the excessively muddy and often impassable road that ran down to the lake from Willoughby. The families between the lake and town were often unable to travel on this road to go to town or attend church services. So, the local minister compared them to a nation cut off from the rest of the world, Lost Nation.

STRAWBERRY SHORTCAKE INVENTION

A dessert that might be just as American as apple pie might have been invented here in Lake County. Hannah Hall was an early pioneer who came to the Chagrin region in 1812 with her husband and four children. They lived in a log cabin in Willoughby with primitive furniture and only had three cooking utensils, according to her daughter Mary. These included a Dutch oven, a long-handled frying pan and an iron pot.

As the legend goes, Hannah baked a shortcake in the frying pan over a fire in the fireplace in the Hall home. Since wild strawberries grew abundantly nearby, when the shortcake cooled, she topped it with cream and strawberries. According to Mary, she was so pleased with her delicious invention that she wrote to friends in New York to tell them of her discovery, and the recipe quickly became popular across the country.

JOHNNYCAKE RIDGE ROAD

There are a few possible explanations for Johnnycake Ridge Road's unique name. Many older homes are found on the stretch of historic roadway in the north end of Concord Township, running from the Painesville Township line to the Mentor line.

According to archives in Concord's Old Stone Schoolhouse, one story comes from notes found in an old chest that turned up in a secondhand store in Painesville: "The notes indicated that the name Johnnycake Ridge was the result of a practical joke. In 1818, Tobias Williams, a rough and unsteady pioneer stopped at an area tavern and was served Johnnycakes. He was so impressed with the area; he himself opened a tavern in 1819."

Williams Tavern on Route 84 and Morley Road became a familiar stagecoach stop. (It is now privately owned and retains much of the original building, including a handmade stone fireplace at the rear of the house, said to have been used to bake the johnnycakes.)

A sign in front of the tavern read:

Breakfast—Salt Pork, Johnnycake
Lunch—Johnny Cake, Salt Pork
Supper—scraps from breakfast and dinner

The sign became the joke of the neighborhood, and some young folks decided to add to it one night, baking a large Johnnycake and hanging it on the side of the tavern. According to the notes, "The next morning when the stagecoach pulled up, one of the passengers remarked, 'Well, this must be Johnnycake Ridge.' The name stuck and was adopted by officials."

In the schoolhouse, another explanation is noted, saying the name comes from the area's New England roots: "One of the staples that they traveled with to this area was cornmeal from which they made long lasting 'Journey cakes.'" When pronounced with a New England accent, "journey cake" became "johnnycake."

Some say it was named after a tavern found on the route that served johnnycake (cornbread) with breakfast, lunch and dinner. Others say it was named after neighbors who played a joke on a tavern owner who never opened his doors for business, so neighbors hung a johnnycake reinforced with horsehair on his unopened inn.

A recipe for authentic Johnnycakes, courtesy of the Old Stone Schoolhouse:

½ cup flour
1 cup cornmeal
1–2 tablespoons sugar
1 tablespoon salt
1 egg
1 cup hot milk

Mix dry ingredients, stir in remaining ingredients, drop on hot griddle and brown on both sides. Serve with butter and syrup.

Wickliffe Cemetery

Most people don't realize while driving in the west end of Wickliffe that an old cemetery is tucked away behind some buildings.

The Wickliffe Cemetery, behind the Provo House at 28855 Euclid Avenue, is a small cemetery that was established in 1808 and consists of 184 known graves. Headstones are etched with the names of many of the city's earliest settlers, including William and Clarissa Clarke Jones, along with other familiar names, like Arnold, Fuller, Grave, Lloyd, Taylor, Hardaker, King, Strong and Rush.

Grave sites of Civil War veterans span the north slope of the cemetery. The oldest grave is from 1808, and the most recent grave is marked 1978.

The cemetery is open to the public, but according to the City of Wickliffe website, access might be limited in the winter due to snow accumulation. A display board shows a map of the cemetery, and detailed brochures are available from the Wickliffe Area Chamber of Commerce, located inside the Provo House.

Kirtland Temple Graffiti

While driving down Chillicothe Road into the quaint city of Kirtland, a tall, white church looms at the top of the hill. Although many know it as the historic Kirtland Temple, they likely don't know that inside, some of its history is quite literally written on its walls. Many of its founders left their signatures and initials throughout the temple, and others have followed suit over the years.

The Kirtland Temple has been a landmark in Kirtland for nearly two hundred years. It was the first Church of Latter-day Saints temple and was completed between 1833 and 1836. Joseph Smith Jr. and his followers used local sandstone and wood from area forests to build the structure known then as the House of the Lord. At the time, it was one of the largest buildings in northern Ohio.

It was used as a place of worship and for educational purposes. In its early days, more than one hundred Kirtland High School students filled the attic level of the temple to learn their lessons. Another room served as a classroom space for the first Latter-day Saints seminary, and a Hebrew grammar class held at the temple was among the first seminaries in Ohio.

Above: Some of the oldest graves at Wickliffe Cemetery on Euclid Avenue. *Photo courtesy of Willoughby Historical Society.*

Left: The Kirtland Temple. *Courtesy of Library of Congress.*

By 1838, the Kirtland Temple was the center of community life for more than two thousand believers, but just a year later, shortly after the dedication of the temple, only one hundred remained. Both personal and financial tensions between the Kirtland community and the church members escalated. Hundreds of church members moved west, many to Missouri and Illinois.

By 1842, the church community had increased to five hundred members, and today, it remains an important place to visit and tour for both believers and historians. In the 1840s, some of Joseph Smith's original followers began caring for the temple, and the group, known as the Community of Christ, continues to do so today.

The temple and nearby related historic buildings have been restored over the years, which has led to the uncovering of some interesting pieces of history.

Tom Kimball, a staff member at the Kirtland Temple Historic Site, is passionate about its history, partly because he's related to many of its founders. He says this leads to interesting conversations with visitors to the temple because sometimes it turns out that they're related. Kimball says his great-grandmother Vilate Murry Kimball made clothes for temple builders. His great-great-grandfather Joel Hills Johnson built the lumber mill that supplied lumber for the temple. His mother is a Smith, and her ancestry can be traced back to Joseph Smith Jr.

He says it's exciting when he stumbles across a signature from a relative. So far, at least one hundred pieces of historic graffiti have been discovered, with names and initials written on wood and walls with pencil, paint and chalk. Some are even carved or made out of nails hammered into the shapes of letters.

"I find new names and initials almost every time I look," Tom said. "There must be a hundred so far." Tom believes the oldest piece of graffiti is from 1856, found on a post in the top level of the bell tower.

"I believe I have found construction notes in other places, such as those next to the spools in the pillars, that facilitate the veils or curtains that divided the rooms into smaller compartments," Tom explains. "There are two initials found in the middle bell tower that have possible important implications. Joseph Smith's first scribe in translating the Book of Mormon was named Martin Harris. He chose not to follow Joseph west in 1838 and remained in Kirtland for almost forty years."

He also discovered a stylized carving of H.S. that is likely from Joseph Smith's brother, Hyrum Smith.

Tom, who also gives presentations on the historic graffiti he has discovered, says some of the most intriguing pieces of graffiti are written in Italian. The most modern graffiti is from the 1980s, found between the box pews. According to Tom's theory, this falls under the vandalism category, because he believes graffiti is vandalism, unless it's one hundred years old, and then it is interesting.

The question is, why have so many people left their signatures or initials over the years in a place that is sacred for so many?

"To my people, Kirtland is of sorts a slice of the Garden of Eden. When we come here, we can feel something important, special, and we just want a little of whatever that is to just rub off on us," Tom explains. "Something like leaving a stone on a grave of a loved one or shepherds leaving a modest gift for the Christ child. They want something of themselves to stay behind in this holy place."

The Ghost Cat of Fairport Harbor Lighthouse

For centuries, lighthouses have been tied with tales of ghost stories. Many are rumored to be haunted, perhaps by the lightkeeper who returns in spirit to continue their job of guiding stray ships at sea. Or maybe by the ghost of those who have lost their lives in tragic shipwrecks just miles from the beacon on shore.

The Fairport Harbor Lighthouse certainly isn't the first lighthouse to be tied with tales of the paranormal, but it might be the only one believed to be haunted by a cat.

Nearly 150 years ago, in 1871, when Civil War veteran captain Joseph Babcock was the lighthouse's head keeper, he lived with his family on the second floor of what is currently the lighthouse museum. The captain and his wife, Mary, had two children who were born at the lighthouse during his tenure, a daughter and a son, Robbie, who died from smallpox in 1889, when he was just five years old.

Mary became very ill shortly after Robbie's death and was bedridden. Her husband brought her cats to keep her company and help pass the time. He found a gray cat in the basement, and it became one of her favorite feline companions. After Mary died, the cat disappeared.

Keepers lived in the lighthouse dwelling until 1925, and United States Coast Guard officers were the next to reside there. It remained unoccupied until 1945, when curators once again began living in the keeper's dwelling.

In the early '90s, the last lighthouse curator to live on the site, Pamela Brent, was upstairs in the Babcocks' former living quarters. She told people that she had seen glimpses of a gray ghost cat playfully running across the floor near the kitchen, and one night, it even felt like it jumped on the bed and was resting against her. Lighthouse volunteers also spoke of an eerie presence in the historic building.

Then one day in 2001, museum trustees decided to install air conditioning. One of the workers wiggled his way into a narrow crawl space in the basement to install the new system. He felt his head resting on something as he tried to maneuver through and discovered the mummified remains of the gray cat.

Since this discovery, the ghost cat has been featured on local news stories and several national shows, including Animal Planet's *The Haunted*, A&E Biography's *Ghost Stories 2012* and Discovery Channel's *Weird, True and Freaky*.

About ten to fifteen years ago, a name-the-ghost-cat contest was held, and Sentinel was chosen. Sentinel's remains are still in the lighthouse museum for curious visitors to see.

GRAVITY HILL

There are stretches of roads throughout the country known as gravity hill that are usually tied with a mysterious story or creepy legend. Lake County has its own gravity hill but without the strange story to go with it.

It's just plain and simple: drivers who let their car coast in a short section of King Memorial Road in Kirtland Hills, north of Little Mountain Road, feel like they are rolling downhill on what appears to be an uphill road.

Is it an optical illusion, or does it truly defy gravity? Many have tried to figure that out for themselves over the years, however local police prefer that they stop slowly coasting and stick to driving at the posted speed limit.

LEGEND OF THE MELONHEADS

The legend of the melonheads has been around for decades. Although the details in the story vary, depending on who is telling it, one thing remains the same—these human-like beings are said to roam the woods and roads near Wisner Road in Kirtland Hills and Chardon.

Gravity Hill at King Memorial Road, just past Little Mountain Road. *Photo by author.*

Driving around at night searching for melonheads, is a popular pastime for many Lake County teenagers, myself included several decades ago. (Remember those days, my cousin and friends who are reading this?) The goal, of course, is to find a melonhead, confirming the legend, and to scare yourself silly in the process. We, however, only succeeded in the latter.

There are many locals, though, or at least a friend of your hairdresser's third cousin's wife, who swear they have seen a melonhead running through the woods at night with giant heads, huge glowing eyes and razor teeth, standing about four feet tall and looking for their next human or animal to attack. So, what is it that makes melonheads so angry and aggressive?

Well, according to one story, they were people who were subjected to strange experiments through government testing. This resulted in their heads becoming disfigured and enlarged so that they were sent to a secret location in the woods, deep in the Chardon/Kirtland countryside. Every once in a while, a melonhead would wander from the safety and seclusion of their home searching for civilization, and this is when those living nearby caught a glimpse of them. In this story, however, the melonheads are generally afraid of anyone they come across and quickly head back to their homes.

Several other versions are centered on a Dr. Crowe (sometimes spelled Crow). He was believed to subject people who were either kidnapped or acquired through an undercover deal with a mental hospital where he worked to bizarre experiments, mostly involving their heads, and including lobotomies.

In other stories, the experiment subjects are children who suffered from hydrocephalus, a disease that results in an unusual buildup of cerebrospinal fluid in the brain and causes the head to swell. As the story goes, some mean-spirited locals began calling them melonheads, so Dr. Crowe and his wife kept them inside their home in the woods to prevent more ridicule and spare the children's feelings. One day, when Mrs. Crowe passed away, the children, who saw her as a mother, were said to panic and run wildly around the cabin. A lit kerosene lantern was knocked over and set the wooden cabin on fire, along with the children and Dr. Crowe who were inside. In this story, the melonheads are the ghosts of the children who roam the woods at night.

In yet another version, the children Dr. Crowe performed tests on became very angry. They attacked and killed him and burned the cabin down and ran off into the nearby woods.

Crybaby Bridge

For many, Crybaby Bridge is a necessary stop on their journey through "Melonhead Country." According to some locals, if you park on the bridge at night and turn off your car engine, you can hear the cry of the poor melonhead children echoing throughout the woods.

The small bridge crosses over a creek that branches off of the Chagrin River. The bridge is on a very narrow portion of Wisner Road that turns from pavement to dirt once you cross over. The road then dead ends, and the woods are dotted with signs saying, "road closed" and "private property."

Although this portion of the street is lined with dense foliage that covers the road like a canopy in some sections, it is a quiet residential area dotted with beautiful homes and hiking/riding trails, so it's not recommended to stop your car on the bridge to look for melonheads. It's also likely that the "cries" heard under the bridge are just distorted sounds created by the acoustics of running water and wild animals in the deep ravine below.

WILLOUGHBY "FRIENDSHIP WALL"

Although there is a playground at Wes Point Park in downtown Willoughby, children often prefer climbing along a wall of large stones that creates a border on one side of the park.

Above: Crybaby bridge on Wisner Road. *Photo by author.*

Left: The Friendship Wall in downtown Willoughby, with a gazebo in the background and commemorative plaque in the foreground. *Photo by author.*

It is, however, no ordinary wall and was created more than a century ago, when Willoughby mayor W.J. Carmichael lived across the street from the park at 4221 River Street. In 1916–17, Mayor Carmichael, while sitting on his front porch, mentioned he wanted to build a friendship wall in front of his home. He notified the local newspaper, asking friends and citizens to donate rocks to build it.

A plaque at the site reads: "He received so many that it's impossible to name every type of stone. They included a piece from the Great Wall of China, a meteorite, lava rock from Hawaii, and part of a millstone."

The mayor was able to build a wall on the school side of River Street, too, because he received such a surplus of rocks.

Homestead House Bed-and-Breakfast

The Homestead House Bed-and-Breakfast on West Spaulding Street in downtown Willoughby is layered with more than a century of history. It began with Alonzo and Sarah Gunn, who moved into the present-day Pine Ridge Country Club in 1860. Four years later, they started spending winters at the Homestead House property so that their daughters, Lenora and Harriet, could go to nearby schools. They also had a son, Edgar, who passed away while he was still an infant.

Sarah inherited the home, so Alonzo had to sign a document saying she alone owned it and he had no rights to the property, which was extremely rare at the time.

After spending winters there for nearly two decades, the Gunns' home burned to the ground in the early morning hours of November 9, 1883, when a fire, that started a street north of their property blazed through downtown Willoughby.

Alonzo decided to rebuild on the charred rubble of the existing foundation. At the time, he was only living there with one daughter because his wife had died in 1879, and his other daughter had married and moved out. Then in 1912, eleven years after Alonzo died, Harriet sold the family property, got married and moved to Florida.

For the next few decades, the building housed many different businesses, including a brothel and a speakeasy. In 1937, the Independent Order of Odd Fellows, a charitable fraternity that anonymously helped those in need, owned the building. In 1945, the Willoughby Assembly of God had its first

The Homestead House Bed-and-Breakfast building years earlier. *Courtesy of Deanna and Fred Rowe.*

church service in the building and then sold it to the founders of the Fine Arts Association, James and Louise Savage, in the 1950s.

The Savages lived upstairs with their family and used the bottom floor for music, art, theater and dance lessons, charging only for music lessons. In the 1970s, when the Savages built the School of Fine Arts on Mentor Avenue, they sold the West Spaulding building, and it eventually became a ceramics studio. By 2004, the structure was abandoned, had bad water damage and was filled to the ceiling with boxes. The City of Willoughby was preparing to demolish it.

In stepped Deanna Rowe. While shopping at the downtown Willoughby farmer's market, she mentioned to members of the Willoughby Historical Society that she was glad to see the downtown being revitalized and that she'd love to see a bed-and-breakfast added to the mix because she always enjoyed staying at them while traveling as chief financial officer of the Fine Arts Association.

The folks at the historical society said there was a building around the corner that had potential to become a bed-and-breakfast. So, she decided to take a look inside, and when she walked through, it was awful, but she could envision how beautiful it could be if it was restored.

In late 2004, she and her husband, Fred, bought the historic property, and after two and a half years of hard work, they opened to the public. The bed-and-breakfast is known for its historic beauty, prime location and Deanna's delicious made-from-scratch breakfasts. Deanna refers to herself as a recovering accountant and realized after going through her receipts that she has used around 10,000 eggs a year to cook for her guests, adding up to more than 1.5 million eggs since she opened.

Renovating was no easy task. The Rowes discovered the ceiling height in the dirt basement wasn't up to code, so Fred dug out fifteen inches of dirt (moving it to their beautiful flower beds in five-gallon buckets) to adjust the level, which took the whole summer.

While digging, he discovered something unusual—a large, round structure made out of beautiful old bricks that extended far into the ground. While digging behind the building to add a back door (because it only had a side and front door), they found a similar but larger structure with an angled slide

The Homestead House Bed-and-Breakfast. *Photo by author.*

that seemed to lead to the circle in the basement. A historical excavator said it was indeed an interesting discovery. He said the large circle of bricks in the backyard was a cistern used to collect rainwater and melting show, which then went down the slide into the smaller well in the basement, allowing the family to have freshwater in their home year-round, which was essentially unheard of at the time. The Rowes covered the cistern and well with dirt when they continued their renovations but kept a stone that they discovered that used to hold the pump for the cistern.

While digging through the charred rubble in the basement from the fire that destroyed the original building so long ago, the Rowes also found a lot of bottles that had been used for milk, medicine and whiskey (possible remnants from the building's role as a speakeasy).

The Roweses' son, Brandon, even stumbled on a secret door with hinges lying flat on the floor on the second level. When they opened it, they discovered a stairwell, likely an escape route during Prohibition, to the first floor. They had to remove the stairwell to add the kitchen for the bed-and-breakfast, but the hinged door remains in the Speakeasy room, available for guests to reserve.

The Rowes named the bed-and-breakfast the Homestead House after Fred came across Alonzo Gunn's will, leaving his "Homestead House" to his two daughters. Deanna says they believe he might have been referring to the original structure that burned down, which they think was an original Connecticut Land Grant House. To honor one of the home's original families who laid the groundwork for the business they run today, calling it the Homestead House just made sense.

Lake Erie beach at Willoughbeach Amusement Park, early 1900s. *Courtesy of Willoughby Historical Society.*

Epilogue

Lake County began as a vast territory of land brimming with potential. The county was developed over time by brave pioneers, hardworking farmers, fearless leaders and creative inventors. It has a rich history full of hardship, perseverance and triumph. Lake Erie maritime history runs deep in its roots and remains at its heart.

Today, it is thriving with business, agriculture, recreation and art, thanks in part to our county's earliest history-makers. Each generation has contributed something special, adding layers of pivotal history to the Lake County we know and love. Although times have changed, remnants of that early history remain to remind us of our storied past, and Lake County residents continue to be hard-working trailblazers paving the way for future generations.

BIBLIOGRAPHY

Ackerman, Kenneth D. "The Garfield Assassination Altered American History, but Is Woefully Forgotten Today." *Smithsonian Magazine*, November 19, 2018. https://www.smithsonianmag.com.

"Arthur Douglas Baldwin II." *Cleveland Plain Dealer*. https://obits.cleveland.com.

"Biography of Charles A. Otis." Online Biographies. http://www.onlinebiographies.info.

"Black History Month, 2014: The Tuskegee Airmen on Blackpast.org." Blackpast. https://www.blackpast.org.

Brennan's Fish House. History. http://brennansfishhouse.com.

"A Brief History of the Village of Kirtland Hills." Lake County Ohio. https://www.lakecountyohio.gov.

Cambridge Historical Commission. "Frequently Asked Questions." https://www.cambridgema.gov.

Cambridge Historical Society. "Washington Elm Debate Rages On: Fact or Legend?" https://cambridgehistory.org.

Case Western Reserve University. "Everett, Henry A." *Encyclopedia of Cleveland History*. https://case.edu.

———. "Maritime Disasters." *Encyclopedia of Cleveland History*. https://case.edu.

———. "Nike Missile Bases." *Encyclopedia of Cleveland History*. https://case.edu.

———. "Otis, Charles Augustus, Jr." *Encyclopedia of Cleveland History*. https://case.edu.

———. "Pickands Mather & Co." *Encyclopedia of Cleveland History.* https://case.edu.

———. "Polyone Corp." *Encyclopedia of Cleveland History.* https://case.edu.

"The Casement House/General Jack and Frances Jennings Casement." Historical Marker Database. https://www.hmdb.org.

Caver, Joseph, Jerome Ennels and Daniel Haulman. *The Tuskegee Airman: An Illustrated History: 1939–1949.* Montgomery, AL: NewSouth Books, 2011.

"Centennials and Timeline of Medical Education in Central Ohio." https://library.osu.edu.

Chojnacki, Linda. "Brennan's Fish House Showcases the Best in Lake Erie Perch and Walleye." https://www.cleveland.com.

City of Eastlake, Ohio website. https://eastlakeohio.com.

City of Mentor. "Wildwood Cultural Center." https://cityofmentor.com.

City of Wickliffe website. "Coulby Mansion." https://www.cityofwickliffe.com.

———. "History of Wickliffe." https://www.cityofwickliffe.com.

———. "Wickliffe Cemetery." https://www.cityofwickliffe.com.

"The Civil War Letters of John S. Casement." RAAB Collection. https://www.raabcollection.com.

Cleveland Memory Project. "Mentor Harbor Yachting Club." 1955.

Cleveland Museum of Natural History. "Mentor Marsh & Carol H. Sweet Nature Center." https://www.cmnh.org.

Concord Township website. "History: Timeline 1797–Present." https://concordtwp.com.

"Cook Cleland." *Pensacola News Journal.* https://www.legacy.com.

Cunningham, John M. "United States Presidential Election of 1880." Britannica. https://www.britannica.com.

Delaney, David G. "Federal Civil Defense Act of 1950." https://www.encyclopedia.com.

De St. Jorre, John. *Legendary Golf Clubs of the American Midwest.* Wellington, FL: EdgeworthEditions, 2013.

Doenecke, Justus. "James A Garfield: Family Life." University of Virginia. https://millercenter.org.

Dorr, Robert F. "Tuskegee Airmen vs. Me-262s." Defense Media Network. https://www.defensemedianetwork.com.

"Earl Lane in the 1940 Census." Ancestry. https://www.ancestry.com.

"Eerie Presence Found in Lighthouse." NewsNet5. http://www.fairportharborlighthouse.org.

"Everything You Need to Know About the Historic Steel Mansion." Lakehouse Inn. https://thelakehouseinn.com.

Fairport Harbor. "History of Fairport Harbor." https://fairportharbor.org.

Fairport Harbor Lighthouse. https://www.lighthousefriends.com.

Fairport Harbor Marine Museum and Lighthouse. http://www.fairportharborlighthouse.org

"Federal Defense Act of 1950." Homeland Security Digital Library. https://www.hsdl.org.

Felton, Chad. "Aviatrix and Lake County Native Marge Hurlburt Celebrated at Rider's Inn." *News-Herald*, September 26, 2018. https://www.news-herald.com.

————. "Perry Coal & Feed Co. Celebrating Its 100 Year Anniversary." *News-Herald*, September 27, 2018. https://www.news-herald.com.

Forever Missed. "Earl R. Lane." https://www.forevermissed.com.

Fratino, Lou, and Kathy Suglia. "The Lloyd Papers II." *Wickliffe Historical Society* 18, no. 1 (Spring 2008).

Freeman, Paul. "Ohio: Northeastern Cleveland Area." Abandoned and Little-Known Airfields. http://www.airfields-freeman.com.

Ganson, William Rose. *Cleveland: The Making of a City*. Kent, OH: Kent State University Press, 1990.

Green, Jerie Ireland. *The Lake Effect: 200 Years of Business in Lake County*. Willoughby, OH: Lake County Business Journal, 2003.

Greenblatt, Mike. *50th Anniversary Woodstock: Back to Yasgur's Farm*. Stevens Point, WI: Krause Publications, 2019.

Gross, Margaret Geissman. *Dancing on the Table: A History of Lake Erie College*. Burnsville, NC: Celo Valley Books, 1993.

Hall of Valor Project. "Cook Cleland." https://valor.militarytimes.com.

"Harry Coulby Is Dead." *New York Times*, January 19, 1929. https://www.nytimes.com.

Hartman, Cecilia. *Aboard* Tinkerbelle *on Her Run to Glory*. Cleveland Memory Project, 1965. http://www.clevelandmemory.org.

Hiltunen, Lasse O. "American Finn Leaves Legacy." Finnish Heritage Museum. http://finnishheritagemuseum.org.

"History of the Cleveland National Air Races." Cleveland National Air Races. https://www.clevelandairshow.com.

Hitchcock, Elizabeth G. *Jonathan Goldsmith: Pioneer Master Builder in the Western Reserve*. Cleveland, OH: Western Reserve Historical Society, 1980.

Hopkins, J.E. *1850: Death on Erie, The Saga of the* G.P. Griffith. Baltimore, MD: Publish America, 2011.

Independent (Willougbhy, OH), November 9, 1883.

Ischay, Lynn. "Sense of Place: Kleifeld's Restaurant Is a Slice of History." Cleveland. https://www.cleveland.com.

"John 'Jack' Sherwin." *Plain Dealer*. https://obits.cleveland.com.

Johnson, Kathleen. "The Federal Civil Defense Agency (FCDA) Women Defend the Nation (1950)." Cold War Museum. http://www.coldwar.org.

Johnston, Laura. "The Ghost Cat of the Fairport Harbor Lighthouse: An Eerie Erie Story." Rock the Lake. October 31, 2017. http://www.rockthelake.com.

Joo, Johnny. "The Eerie Halls of the Madison Seminary." *Architectural Afterlife* (blog), May 10, 2019. https://architecturalafterlife.com.

Kapsch, Joan, Sue Muehlhauser and Kathie Pohl. *Mentor: The First 200 Years*. Mentor, OH: Mentor Bicentennial Committee/Old Mentor Foundation, 1997.

Kay Halle Personal Papers. John F. Kennedy Presidential Library and Museum Archives. https://www.jfklibrary.org.

Kirtland Country Club. "About Us: Club History." https://www.kirtlandcc.org.

Kirtland Country Club. Willoughby, OH: N.p., 1927.

Kirtland Temple. "History." https://www.kirtlandtemple.org.

Lake County Genealogical Society. "Waite Hill Cemetery." https://www.lcgsohio.org.

———. "Wickliffe Pioneer Cemetery." https://www.lcgsohio.org.

Lake County Historical Society. "Here Is Ohio's Lake County: A Historical Journey…Then and Now." 2014.

———. "Appointment Calendar: Lake County Then and Now." 1994.

Lake County History Center. "Celebrating Mayors of Fairport." http://lakehistorycenter.org.

———. "Lake County History Nursery Capital of the World." http://lakehistorycenter.org.

———. "Unionville Tavern." http://lakehistorycenter.org.

Lake County, Ohio website. http://www.lakecountyohio.org.

Lake Erie College. https://www.lec.edu.

Lakeland Community College. "Mooreland Mansion." https://www.lakelandcc.edu.

"Leonard Skeggs (1918–2002)." Science Museum. http://broughttolife.sciencemuseum.org.

"Leonard T." *News-Herald*, December 6, 2002. https://www.news-herald.com.

"Leonard T. Skeggs, PhD." AACC. https://www.aacc.org.

"Library History in Photos: On the Move." Mentor Public Library. http://www.mentorpl.org.

Lillback, Elaine. "Dr. Amy Kaukonen Visits with Lisa Potti Profughi." Finnish Heritage Museum. http://finnishheritagemuseum.org.

Lippucci, Gale. "Willowick History Project." Willoughby-Eastlake Public Library. https://we247.org.

Lloyd, James T. *Lloyd's Steamboat Directory, and Disasters on the Western Waters.* Cincinnati, OH: James T. Lloyd & Co., 1856.

Lupold, Harry Forrest. *The Latch String Is Out: A Pioneer History of Lake County, Ohio.* Mentor, OH: Lakeland Community College Press, 1974.

"Madison Seminary Ghost Hunt." Haunted Explorations Events. http://hauntedexplorationsevents.com.

Malonee, Laura. "Venture into a Surreal Salt Mine 2,000 Feet Below Lake Erie." Wired, May 3, 2016. https://www.wired.com.

Manry, Robert. *Tinkerbelle.* New York: Harper and Row, 1965.

Mansfield, John Brandt. *History of the Great Lakes: Illustrated.* Chicago: N.p., 1899.

Maritime History of the Great Lakes. "G.P. Griffith (Steamboat), 18 Oct 1847." http://images.maritimehistoryofthegreatlakes.ca.

———. "G.P. Griffith (Steamboat), burnt, 17 June 1850." http://images.maritimehistoryofthegreatlakes.ca.

———. "G.P. Griffith (Steamboat,) Collision, 17 Oct. 1849." http://images.maritimehistoryofthegreatlakes.ca.

Matowitz, Thomas G., Jr. *Mentor.* Charleston, SC: Arcadia Publishing, 2015.

Maxson, Dan. "Concord Notables." *Local Lore* (blog). http://wwwnews-heraldcom.blogspot.com.

———. "Lost Airfields of Lake County—Cook Cleland Airport." *Local Lore* (blog). http://wwwnews-heraldcom.blogspot.com.

———. "Willowick-Opoly." Lake History Center. http://lakehistorycenter.org.

———. "You Might Be from Lake County If." *Local Lore* (blog). http://wwwnews-heraldcom.blogspot.com.

McKendree Avery, Elroy. *A History of Cleveland and Its Environs: The Heart of New Connecticut.* Vol. 3. Chicago: Lewis Publishing Company, 1918.

McMahon, Marian. "Two Special Women Inducted into Hall of Fame." Gazette Newspapers, June 12, 2017. http://www.gazettenews.com.

Michaud, Denise, and the Madison Historical Society. *Madison.* Charleston, SC: Arcadia Publishing, 2010.

Moore, Rose. "The Story of Marge Hurlburt and the Women of WASP." *Rose About Town* (blog), December 29, 2013. http://www.roseabouttown.com.

Mount Holyoke. "History: Go Where No One Else Will." https://www.mtholyoke.edu.

Mountain Creek Tree Farm. "About Us." http://mountaincreektrees.com.

New York Times News Service. "Kay Halle, Glamorous Heiress Who Captivated the Powerful." August 24, 1997. https://www.chicagotribune.com.

Ohio Department of Natural Resources. "Mentor Marsh State Nature Preserve." https://naturepreserves.ohiodnr.gov.

Ohio History Central. "Lake County." http://www.ohiohistorycentral.org.

———. "The Madison Home: From a Grand Army to Ghosts." https://ohiohistoryhost.org.

———. "Ohio's State Mammal—White Tailed Deer." https://ohiohistorycentral.org.

Ohio History Connection. "The Casement House." https://remarkableohio.org.

———. "Go to 24-43 Harry Coulby Marker Home." http://www.remarkableohio.org.

———. "Robert Manry After Solo Atlantic Ocean Crossing." https://ohiomemory.org.

Ohio Wine Producers Association. "Vines & Wines Vine Trail." https://www.ohiowines.org.

Otis, Charles Augustus. *Here I Am*. Cleveland, OH: Buehler Printcraft, 1951.

Overman, William Daniel. *Ohio Town Names*. Akron, OH: Atlantic Press, 1902.

Oyler Stith, Bari. "History of Geauga County." https://www.co.geauga.oh.us.

Pape, Patricia A. *Legacy of Resilience*. Bloomington, IN: AuthorHouse, 2011.

Podolak, Janet. "As Rider's Inn Celebrates 200 Years of History, Owner Elaine Crane Shares Anecdotes." *News-Herald*, January 29, 2012. https://www.news-herald.com.

———. "History of Mooreland Mansion Stretches to Lake 1800s." *News-Herald*, April 2, 2015. https://www.news-herald.com.

Polmar, Norman. "A Very Able Mariner." U.S. Naval Institute. https://www.usni.org.

Rabbit Run Community Arts Association. "Historic Barn Theater." https://www.rabbitrunonline.org.

Remarkable Lake County, OH. "Willoughby." https://www.mylakeoh.com.

Rolf, Eleanor Gaines. *Willoughby Then and Now 1835–1985*. Willoughby, OH: N.p., 1985.

Scott, Betsy. "Mentor Matchworks Building Back in Business with New Restaurant." *News-Herald*, April 8, 2017. https://www.news-herald.com.

Shankland, Frank N. *Historical Willoughby: 1853 Centennial Celebration 1953*. Willoughby, OH: Willoughby Chamber of Commerce, 1953.

Shofar, Cassandra. "Historical Traffic Signal Replica to be Unveiled in Downtown Willoughby." *News-Herald*, May 12, 2011. https://www.news-herald.com.

Smith, J.Y. "Kay Halle, Washington Grande Dame Dies at 93." *Washington Post*, August 12, 1997. https://www.washingtonpost.com.

"S/S Samaria (2.)" Norway-Heritage. http://www.norwayheritage.com.

Steele Mansion. "About Us." https://www.steelemansion.com.

Stith, Bari Oyler. *Lake County Ohio: 150 Years of Tradition*. Northridge, CA: Windsor Publication, 1988.

Sumner, Keene. *The American Magazine*. New York: Crowell Publishing Company, 1923.

Taddeo, Ronald J. "How Willoughby Got Its Name." City of Willoughby, Ohio. https://willoughbyohio.com.

This Day in Aviation. "13 January 1949." https://www.thisdayinaviation.com.

Thomas, Robert McG, Jr. "Kay Halle, 93, an Intimate of Century's Giants." *New York Times*, August 24, 1997. https://archive.nytimes.com.

Thompson, Mark L. *Graveyard of the Lakes*. Detroit, MI: Wayne State University Press, 2000.

Tryon Curtis, Lillie. "The Story of Waite Hill." Village of Waite Hill, Ohio. http://www.waitehilloh.gov.

"Tuskegee Airmen." History. https://www.history.com.

"The Tuskegee Airmen: 5 Fascinating Facts." History. https://www.history.com.

Unionville, Ohio website. https://www.unionvilleohio.org.

Unionville Tavern Preservation Society. "The Old Tavern." http://www.savethetavern.org.

Van Rensselaer Wickham, Gertrude. *Pioneer Women of the Western Reserve*. Vol. 1. Cleveland, OH: Woman's Department of the Cleveland Centennial Commission, 1896.

Voulgaris, Barbara. "From Steamboat Inspection Service to U.S. Coast Guard: Marine Safety in the United States from 1838–1946." U.S. Department of Defense. https://media.defense.gov.

Waite Hill Land Conservancy. http://www.waitehilloh.gov.

Warth Mills Project. "The Tragedy of the SS *Arandora*." https://www. warthmillsproject.com.

Weber, Cathi. *Haunted Willoughby, Ohio*. Charleston, SC: The History Press, 2010.

Weird U.S. "Melonheads Creep Through the Ohio Woods at Night." http:// www.weirdus.com.

———. "Mentor's Gravity Hill Pulls Them In (And Up)." http://www. weirdus.com.

Western Reserve Historical Society. "What Is the Western Reserve?" https:// www.wrhs.org.

Western Reserve Land Conservancy. https://www.wrlandconservancy.org.

Wheeler, Edward J., and Frank Crane. *Current Opinion Vol LXXIII July– December 1922*. New York: Current Literature Publishing Company, 1922.

Wilkinson, Christina L. *Willoughby*. Charleston, SC: Arcadia Publishing, 2012.

Williams Brothers. *History of Geauga and Lake Counties, Ohio, with Illustrations and Biographical Sketches of its Pioneers and Most Prominent Men*. Philadelphia, PA: J.B. Lippincott, 1878.

Willough Beach Park. https://rcdb.com.

Willoughby Area Welcome Center. "History." https://www. willoughbyareawelcomecenter.com.

Willoughby News Herald Newspaper Archives. https://newspaperarchive. com.

"Willoughby's First Traffic Signal." *Lake County Today*, February 14, 2011. http://lakeco.locable.com.

WKYC Staff. "Underground Rail Road." Rider's Inn. http://www. ridersinn.com.

Works Progress Administration. *Lake County History*. Lake County, OH: Western Reserve Historical Society, Lake County Chapter, 1941.

World Golf Hall of Fame. "Bobby Jones." http://www.worldgolfhalloffame. org.

Worrel, Chris M. "Author Discusses Deadly 1850 Lake Erie Shipping Disaster." Cleveland, January 12, 2019. https://www.cleveland.com.

Wystrach, Steve. *Manry at Sea: In the Wake of a Dream*. 13 1/2 Foot Films LLC, 2018.